CHAOS PARADIGM

A Theological Exploration

Morris A. Inch

University Press of America,® Inc.
Lanham • New York • Oxford

Copyright © 1998
University Press of America,® Inc.
4720 Boston Way
Lanham, Maryland 20706

12 Hid's Copse Rd.
Cummor Hill, Oxford OX2 9JJ

Library of Congress Cataloging-in-Publication Data

Inch, Morris A.
Chaos paradigm : a theological exploration / Morris A. Inch.
p.   cm.
Includes bibliographical references and index.
1. Theology, Doctrinal. 2. Chaos (Christian theology) I. Title.
BT78.I48   1998   230'.01 —dc21   98-9567 CIP

ISBN 0-7618-1060-9 (cloth: alk. ppr.)
ISBN 0-7618-1061-7 (pbk: alk. ppr.)

⊖™The paper used in this publication meets the minimum
requirements of American National Standard for information
Sciences—Permanence of Paper for Printed Library Materials,
ANSI Z39.48—1984

Contents

Acknowledgment   v

Introduction   vii

Chaos from a Biblical Theology Perspective: 1
An Initial Survey--Part I
Tohu and *Bohu* (3), The Deluge (7), Out of Bondage (11),
Bemidbar (15), The Promised Land (19), Chaotic Time of
The Judges (23), Making of the Monarchy (27), Tale of
Two Kingdoms (31), Trauma of Exile (35), Constructive
Approach to Chaos (39), Silence of God (43), The Future
Now (47), Master of Chaos (51), Once For All (55), Life
Together (59), Light and Darkness (63), *Maranatha* (67),
Epilogue (71).

Chaos from a Systematic Theology Perspective: 75
Select Instances--Part II
Chaos Anthropology (77), Chaos Pneumatology (89)

Chaos from a Historical Theology Perspective: 103
A Case Study--Part III
The City of God (105)

Endnotes   119

Bibliography   123

Index   127

Acknowledgment

I should like to express a general word of appreciation to all those who have encouraged me to question over the years. I would add a special word of appreciation to my beloved wife Joan for formatting the text, along with the apt prompting of our son Thomas.

Introduction

Chaos theory has been creating a considerable stir in a wide variety of circles. Any standard university library catalogue will reveal an impressive assortment of representative book titles, ranging from such disciplines as quantum physics to marketing theory. Amazon Books, which serves the Internet, lists several hundred titles. Leon Chua concludes there has never been a phenomenon so ubiquitous, a paradigm so universal, or a discipline so multi-disciplinary.[1]

Succinctly put, the chaos paradigm suggests that order gives way to chaos, and the reverse. It is a function of nonlinear (complex) systems, where fractals (similarities) occur within set boundaries, with a high degree of sensitivity to initial conditions. Commentators characteristically opt to illustrate rather than rely solely on abstract discussion. This seems better to serve their conviction that the chaos paradigm describes life as we encounter it. It is decidedly not something artificially imposed.

The kneading of dough serves as a favorite example. Reality in chaos perspective resembles the process of stretching dough and folding it over, repeated time and again. We may be able to set some parameters on the results, but not the particular set--since initial variables will be multiplied many times over.

We are introduced to chaos at the outset of the Biblical record when it is said that "the earth was formless and empty" (Gen. 1:2). The same expression was employed by Jeremiah to describe the results of the Babylonian invasion: "I looked at the earth, and it was formless and empty" (Jer. 4:23). The resulting social disarray coupled with physical destruction brought to mind the original chaos condition.

Chaos in theological circles has received relatively little attention. Bernard Anderson's *Creation Versus Chaos* (1967) is a notable exception. Written from a historical-critical perspective, it was published well before the rise of contemporary chaos theory.

This is not the case with Ben Carter's *Unity in Diversity* (1991), and John Polkinghorne's *Quarks, Chaos, and Christianity* (1997). These have broken ground in the dialogue between chaos theory and theology.

Theological articles have been more numerous, but still quite limited in number and scope. They characteristically appear tentative, as if feeling their way in unfamiliar surroundings. Conversely, they appear optimistic as to the eventual outcome.

Biblical and religious encyclopedia, so far as I have been able to determine, treat the topic of chaos in a cursory fashion--if at all. They make no mention of chaos theory or its possible relevance.

Taking all into consideration, there is not much precedent and no actual competition for the present work. We explore chaos in three connections: Biblical, systematic, and historical theology. First, a brief survey of the chaos weave in Biblical narrative; second, in more systematic fashion concerning our understanding of man and the Holy Spirit; finally, as represented by Augustine's *magnum opus--The City of God.*

This comes in the form of a progress report. As such, it may be said to resemble the field report of an archaeologist at the conclusion of his/her season of excavation. I hope that there will be other seasons, and shared insights with those engaged in the project. Whether this will prove to be the case of not, I am convinced that we have discovered something of major significance. I am equally persuaded that it comes as no surprise to the Almighty, from whom no secret is withheld.

Part I

Chaos From A Bibilical Theology Perspective: An Initial Survey

Biblical theology as a distinct discipline dates from an article by J.F. Gabler in 1787. His intent was to single out the study of theology in the context of Biblical (hence historical) narrative. Good intentions aside, the effort has been plagued by the rationalism in which it was conceived and nurtured.

Even so, both liberal and conservative scholars have taken an interest in Biblical theology. Whereas the former are inclined to accent the diversity of Scripture, often to the point of contradiction; the latter emphasize its underlying continuity, sometimes at the expense of significant differences. Most would at least in theory agree that we err by accenting either diversity or unity to the exclusion of the other.

Biblical theology considers theology *in situ*, where it occurs in its revelatory process. Otherwise put, it follows a *line* of development. In contrast, systematic theology creates what may be thought of as a *circle,* embracing its data within a systematic whole. There is nonetheless an incipient order to Biblical theology. It is not of the kind we associate with a nursery. It more resembles what we discover as we walk a nature trail.

We set ourselves to track chaos in its Biblical setting. We will be selective in the passages chosen, and use constraint in our commentary. We aim at an overview that can be confirmed, corrected, and expanded. Some may feel we have gone too far, and others not far enough. If the criticism is roughly divided, we will perhaps have achieved our intended purpose. That is, to open the area of Biblical theology to the searchlight of chaos reality.

TOHU AND *BOHU*

"Now the earth was formless (*tohu*) and empty (*bohu*), darkness was over the surface of the deep, and the Spirit of God was hovering over the waters" (Gen. 1:2). This combination of terms (*tohu* and *bohu*) occurs only here and in Jeremiah 4:23, the former with reference to nature and the latter extended to incorporate the disintegration of the social order following the Babylonian invasion..

Tohu is used by itself elsewhere to describe a trackless waste, swept clean by howling winds (Deut. 32:10). Job consequently portrayed his irritating associates as caravans that turn away from their appointed routes into the wasteland and perish (6:18).

The creation narrator obviously intends us to understand *tohu/bohu* as a physical description of the way things were in their initial state. This along with chaos theory mean to describe real conditions, differ as they might in other respects. While not inviting, chaos appears as if the first step in the creative process. As such, it is similar to many other High God traditions. These resemble the potter who casts his clay before refining it into a vessel for use. No value judgement appears intended at this initial point in the narrative, except by way of comparison to subsequent developments.

God's Spirit hovered over the waters, as would an eagle over her cherished brood. We later read how God took care of Israel in the wilderness "like an eagle that stirs its nest and hovers over its young, that spreads its wings to catch them and carries them on its pinions" (Deut. 32:11). God works through chaotic means to accomplish His ultimate purpose.

Gordon Wenham comments: "This frightening disorganization is the antithesis to the order that characterized the work of creation when it was complete....The same point is made in another powerful image in the next clause, 'darkness covered the deep'."[2] Whereas light is introduced in connection with God, darkness comes to represent everything adverse to

Him: wickedness, self-deception, and death--with resulting judgement.

Darkness is one of several initial *referents* (allusions) to chaos. It serves along with silence, the waters, and shortly with death to bring to mind chaos imagery. These are used on occasion either individually or in some combination. As such, they may substitute for chaos, or explore it in some connection or another. Taken together, they suggest how pervasive chaos reality is in the Biblical narrative. Listed separately, they reveal the complex character of chaos as a condition of life and life itself.

Derek Kidner moves the discussion along with the observation that "if God alone brings form out of formlessness, He alone sustains it."[3] Otherwise, we may anticipate the return of chaos in the form of natural disasters, political reverses, social disintegration, and personal disorientation. Jeremiah was therefore on target when applying chaos imagery to the traumatic aftermath of the Babylonian invasion.

God created man in His likeness, which excludes reducing him to anything less or elevating him to something greater. Biblical man is not the product of blind energy but purposeful design. His affinity to other creatures ought not obscure the fact that he was created in God's likeness, to commune with His creator and serve as steward over His creation.

No less is man qualified to join a pantheon. He lacks the comprehensive knowledge, innate capability, and moral rectitude to play god. Whenever he steps out of role, either via reduction or deification, he reaps chaos.

Is there a destiny that guides our way, or are we free to soar like the birds through the heavens? Probably both in chaos perspective. Such randomness as we experience appears to be within some fixed order, ill-perceived as it may often be. Chaos theorists seem agreed on this point.

Man's stance before God took on the form of vocation, permission, and prohibition. While we are inclined to emphasize the last, its significance becomes evident only in connection with the others. *Vocation* refers to man's stewardship of creation. As individuals, we assume this responsibility in some connection or another. We best serve by fulfilling our particular calling with diligence and zeal, and encouraging others to do the same.

Whenever we fail in our calling or intrude on the calling of others, the social order breaks down. As Martin Luther observed, every calling is so demanding that we must give our full attention to it if we are to succeed.

Permission extended to all the fruit of the garden but one. It was a most generous provision. Man lacked nothing that would contribute to his well-being, or enable him to fulfil his calling.

Life, in creation perspective, is good and meant to be enjoyed. As sometimes put, evil is good gone wrong. It is only as we pervert God's purposes that life turns sour.

Prohibition forbade eating of *the tree of the knowledge of good and evil*, with the explanation that should Adam do so he would most assuredly die (Gen. 2:17). The opposites *good and evil* appear idiomatic for *all things* (cf. 24:50; 31:24,29). Thus to usurp knowledge of good and evil was to exceed his critical limits, and reach for autonomy. Reaching higher, man would fall lower still.

We are told that God alone is inherently immortal (1 Tim. 6:16). Man had access to the tree of life in communion with Him. Once man defected, the Almighty removed him from the garden lest he eat and perpetuate an intolerable situation. As God had promised, Adam's days were numbered.

Chaos has been variously illustrated. As often noted, smoke as it ascends into the air thins and vanishes. More representative of the Biblical account, life loses vitality until gone and consumed by the earth. All that was and might have been returns to dust, to formless matter.

Even now we sense death pressing in on us: in the form of personal illness or social indifference. Chaos never seems far removed, and awaits us at the end of our life's journey.

As for now, we live by God's grace as a profligate race in a broken world. Robert Seltzer painfully reflects: We discover a series of stories in which the world, created by a benevolent deity and containing one creature made in His image,

> turns out full of violent, murderous, and self-glorifying men. The state of affairs, in turn, leads to the formation of people nurtured by God, capable of producing a few individuals of satisfactory spiritual nature, but in the main those who are obtuse, unfaithful, and frequently backsliding from the divinely given task.[4]

The character of original sin has been variously explained: as biological, sociological, or religious. If biological, then through genetic means. If sociological, then via social institutions. If religious, then with Adam as representative of the human race.

Chaos theory, as applied to the above, would seem to accent the *essential* character of life (not necessarily to the exclusion of other factors). Edgar Peters elaborates:

> Chaos has shown us that, in natural systems, events can change the course of

history, even if the total number of possible results is within a finite space. ...From a sociological point of view, we can say that certain events must have changed the course of history, even if society does not remember when those events occurred.[5]

Life went on, not triumphantly but somehow. God made provision for man in his fallen condition. In addition, there was a veiled promise associated with the *protoevangelium*: the seed of woman would bruise the serpent's head (Gen. 3:15). This appears from one perspective as providential, and another as redemptive. The former concerns God's initiative, and the latter as to its success. Taken together, they remind us of God's sovereignty and compassion. They are as if a religious commentary on what chaos theorists see as the deterministic character of life.

The *tohu/bohu* formula also reminds us of the fragile character of life as we experience it. It is bad enough that we pollute our environment and trivialize relationships in violation of our stewardship responsibilities, but to reject God who is the source and sustenance of life amounts to utter folly. All that keeps creation from slipping back into primordial chaos is God's mercy and grace. Jonathan Edward's famed sermon *Sinners in the Hands of an Angry God* never seemed more persuasive than in chaos perspective!

THE DELUGE

Things turned from bad to worse. "The Lord saw how great man's wickedness on the earth had become, and that every inclination of the thoughts of his heart was only evil all the time" (6:15). The sin was expansive (*great in the earth*), deeply-rooted (*every imagination of the thoughts of his heart*), in full sway (*only evil*), and unrelenting (*all the day*). Every base seems covered.

This is the classic example of sensitivity to initial conditions. It reaches back to the dim dawn of human society, where sin skewed life from that point on. It developed as one would fold dough over and over, until it took some unpredictable form.

"The Lord was grieved that he had made man on the earth, and his heart was filled with pain" (v. 6). Man no longer fulfilled the purpose for which he had been created, but rather resembled some cosmic contagion.

Still, things continued on much as usual, as if nothing were amiss. "People were eating and drinking, marrying and giving in marriage" (Matt. 24:38). It resembled the proverbial *quiet before the storm*.

It was as if the celestial Potter were pausing to reflect on His marred vessel. No longer suitable, it must be cast aside to make way for another. There remained no creative alternative.

There was one notable exception: "Noah found favor in the eyes of the Lord" (v. 8). He was one of those *few individuals of satisfactory spiritual nature* referred to earlier by Seltzer. He was blameless among his contemporaries, and walked faithfully with God. So when God determined to bring an end to the wicked generation, He directed Noah to build an ark to the saving of his family.

Noah did as God had commanded him, and when the ark was completed, God shut him and his family in. After this, "the springs of the great deep burst forth, and the floodgates of the heavens were opened" (7:11). "The waters above and below the firmament are, in token, merged again, as if to reverse the very work of creation and bring back the featureless waste of waters."[6] Qualifications notwithstanding, the world had returned to its initial chaotic state.

Here as elsewhere, the narrator calls attention to a similarity between spiritual and physical conditions. As concerns the former, sin had inundated the human race. As concerns the latter, the waters would follow suit.

In chaos terms, the conditions appear as self-similar. They bear a fractal relationship within a bounded system..

The ark and those within stand in sharp contrast. They ride the crest of the waves. While chaos rages without, confidence reigns within. God promises a new beginning with life-sustaining order.

A providential nuance becomes obvious in this interplay of chaos and order. Paul picks up this theme at a later time with the observation: "And we know that in all things God works for the good of those who love him, who have been called according to his purpose" (Rom. 8:28). As sometimes stated, "its darkest just before the dawn."

Hebrews employs the building of the ark as an indication of Noah's fear of and faith in God (11:7). He had *time* for God, whereas others were caught up in the daily routine of life; he put *effort* into God's service, while others looked critically on; he *considered* God's word, when others turned a deaf ear; he *obeyed* in the midst of a rebellious people.

We have with Noah the first explicit mention of a *covenant*. A covenant is essentially an agreement implying reciprocal obligations.

Even so, a covenant with God is distinctive. It resembles a *royal covenant,* i.e., between a king and his people. In such instances, the ruler sets the conditions. The people are then obligated to obey, and the ruler to sustain them on condition of their obedience.

This particular covenant "is remarkable for its breadth (embracing 'every living creature'), its permanence ('perpetual', 'everlasting', etc.) And its generosity--for it was unconditional as it was undeserved."[7] It detailed how life henceforth could be perpetuated, secured, and assured of God's blessing. Jewish scholars have further developed its implications concerning idolatry, blasphemy, murder, sexual relations, theft, human treatment of animals, and the establishing of courts of law to carry out justice and maintain morality. It would also seem to account for the requirements set forth at the Jerusalem Council for gentile converts (Acts 15:29).

The covenants structure life in God's world, given the conditions that pertain at the time and with view for the future. Those who abide by their provisions can expect to experience God's blessing. If not, they can expect chaotic times ahead. There are no other alternatives.

God designated the rainbow (resembling a war bow lifted overhead in peace) as His pledge never again to bring so comprehensive a judgment upon the world. He would henceforth postpone judgement sufficient to allow history to run its course. Chaos would be kept on a shorter leash.

Nonetheless, we are reminded that God's Spirit will not continually contend with man (6:3). We ought not to presume on His mercy nor act so as to offend Him. His judgments are right; He calls us to accountability when we little expect it. Time emphatically does not favor the procrastinator.

OUT OF BONDAGE

Genesis closes with Israel little more than an extended family enjoying the patronage of Egypt; Exodus commences with her greatly increased in numbers and as a reported threat to the current regime. "While it is perhaps a possibility that the 'sons of Israel' in the delta may outnumber their Egyptian overlords at the beginning of a relocation there of Egyptian power, the likelier explanation is that the king of Egypt is reported as justifying his severe forced labor policies by recourse to scare tactics."[8] In any case, the Pharaoh who *knew not Joseph* set task-masters over the people, forcing them to work in the fields and in building his store cities.

When the children of Israel continued to propagate, the Pharaoh ordered the Hebrew mid-wives to destroy all male children at birth. When the mid-wives failed to cooperate, he commanded that such children as might escape be cast into the Nile. Genocide was the order of the day.

Slavery as experienced by those subject to it is chaotic. They are not allowed to structure life for themselves; others usurp that privilege. Such indulgences as they wee granted could as easily be withdrawn. They were tossed about as if a piece of drift-wood on the turbulent waves.

Bondage is most difficult to manage when religiously sanctioned. The Egyptians cultivated an extensive pantheon.

> In the earliest days each village in Egypt looked to its own deity for the blessings of life and protection against hostile powers, human or demonic. The village would boast a shrine to its deity, and the worship of the local god served as a unifying influence within the community and a means of distinguishing one village from another.[9]

As the communities combined to become states, some gods and goddesses prospered at the expense of others. With the unification of Egypt, the Pharaoh was elevated to the pantheon. He was said to be the incarnation and patron of the falcon god Horus, associated with the sun and perpetually doing battle with his evil brother Seth--the storm god.

As priest for and participant in the pantheon, what Pharaoh willed was *ipso facto* the will of the gods. Conversely, to challenge Pharaoh was to take on an awesome assembly of deities. The Hebrew people had the religious cult stacked against them.

While the plagues may have appeared as simply a contest between Moses and the Pharaoh, they were in effect an assault on the chaotic perpetrators of the Egyptian pantheon. Christoph Barth comments:

> Tales about the Creator's victory express what Israel knew as God's saving act at the beginning of its own history. Pharaoh and his army were for Israel a terrible incarnation of chaotic forces. Not by chance, but by virtue of the Lord's victory, Israel escaped them. The Red Sea victory was thus a solid basis for belief in the Creator's initial victory over all the forces of chaos and evil.[10]

The threat of genocide was simply the final solution to the dehumanizing process of slavery. Stripped of their rights, the Hebrew people could as easily be deprived of life--if it served the purposes of their oppressors.

There comes to mind the story of Jewish prisoners herded out of cattle cars into processing sheds during World War II. One clutched a prized manuscript, the fruit of years of labor. A menacing guard tore it from his grasp and gleefully cast it into a pile of rubble. Then, he pulled off the man's thickly-ground glasses, and crushed them under his heel. He was content for the moment; he would leave the rest for the gas ovens to consume. Such is the brutality that survives in our world to the present century, justified to perpetuate an Aryan race--as a delusion fostered by barbarian gods.

Moses was tending his father-in-law's flock on the far side of the desert, as it approached *the mountain of God*. There he saw a strange phenomenon, a burning bush that was not consumed. When he drew closer, God spoke to him from the bush and appointed him to deliver the Hebrew people from bondage.

If they should ask: "What is his name?" Moses inquired. "Then what shall I tell them?" (Exod. 3:13).

> To ask the question, "Under what new title has God appeared to you" is equivalent to asking, "What new revelation have you received from God?" Normally, in patriarchal days, any new revelation of the ancestral god will be

summed up in a new title for Him (Gen. 16:13) which will in future both record and recount a deeper knowledge of God's saving activity.[11]

Yahweh (I am or will be) came by way of answer. Variously explained, R. Alan Cole concludes:

Perhaps the easiest way to understand what the name YHWH meant to the Jews is to see what it came to mean, as their history of salvation slowly unrolled. It ultimately meant to them what the name Jesus has come to mean to Christians, a 'shorthand' for all God's dealings of grace.[12]

God awaits us at each point along life's way, there to minister to our need. Then, when redemptive history has run it course, He awaits us still. Dale Aukerman pertinently comments:

Hope for the consummation is not an addition or a complement to other hoping. It is the keystone; all other hopes should lean toward it. No other hope, cause, or movement, however important for the human future, is to be given that central place.[13]

Hope seems in principle vindicated in chaos perspective. Order as we have known it lapses into chaos, only to return in some creative fashion. Life goes on for those who do not despair, but trust their ways to God.

Still, we are cautioned not to put our trust in some transitory feature of life. The kingdoms man builds, time and circumstance bring to ruin. This recalls the musings of Percy Bysshe Shelley:

I met a traveler from an antique land
Who said: Two vast and trunkless legs of stone
Stand in the desert... . Near them, on the sand,
Half sunk, a shattered visage lies, whose frown,
And wrinkled lip, and sneer of cold command,
Tell that is sculptor well those passions read
Which yet survive, stamped on these lifeless things,
The hand that mocked them, and the heart that fed:
And on the pedestal these words appear:
"My name is Ozymandias, king of kings:
Look on my works, ye Mighty, and despair!"
Nothing beside remains. Round decay
Of that colossal wreck, boundless and bare
The lone and level sands stretch far away.

Ozymandias was the Greek name for Ramses II, thought by some the pharaoh who oppressed the Hebrew people. Shelley, always the ardent advocate of the oppressed, meant to reproach those who would enslave others to further their own ambition.

Hosea anticipated Shelley's complaint. He cautioned that of those who "sow the wind and reap the whirlwind" (8:7). That is, they reap what they sow and worse, as would a storm build with the passing of time. Nonlinear systems, it bears repeating, are sensitive to initial conditions.

BEMIDBAR

The Hebrews took their leave of Sinai, where they received and ratified their covenant treaty. They were bound for the promised land, and sent representatives of the tribes ahead to explore Canaan. See what the land is like; whether the people who live there are strong or weak, few or many; what sort of towns they live in, whether unprotected or fortified (Num. 13:18-20).

The spies reported back that the land was indeed rich and productive, but the inhabitants strong and their cities well guarded. Caleb confidently urged: "We should go up and take possession of the land for we can certainly do it." But others warned: "We cannot attack those people; they are stronger than we are."

"Appalled by the spies' description of the promised land, the people break down completely."[14] The community of faith so carefully molded at Sinai unraveled before their eyes. There was talk of returning to Egypt and bondage rather than accept the challenge of freedom.

God's anger was kindled.

As surely as I live and as surely as the glory of the Lord fills the whole earth, not one of the men who saw my glory and the miraculous signs I performed in Egypt and in the desert but who disobeyed me and tested me ten times--not one of them will ever see the land I promised on oath to their forefathers (14:21-23).

The fate they had feared upon entry into the promised land would overtake them in the wilderness (*bemidbar*).

The wilderness is by definition a desolate place. Jeremiah referred to it as "a land not sown" (2:2). Job compared the plight of the poor with wild donkeys in the desert (24:5), seeing both have to scrounge for survival. The wilderness provided little water and few inhabited it (cf. Job 38:25-27). "In short, the desert is opposed to inhabited land as a curse is opposed to blessing."[15]

Thus the wilderness joins other referents to chaos. Its bare features resemble the formless void at the dawn of creation. There is little to resemble the rich flora and fauna which came to be as the result of God's continuing activity.

The wilderness nevertheless comes to have contrasting nuances. First, as the way to the land of promise. In this regard, it recalls the process of creation--with chaos and then order. Whatever problems we associate with chaos, it can be a creative step toward subsequent order.

Second, since the wilderness sojourn was extended as the result of disbelief, it came to represent experiencing the wrath of God. "As the years of the desert sojourn passed, each one would remind the survivors of Israel's supreme act of rebellion against the Lord of the covenant."[16] As subsequent generations came and went, they would back on this event as a grim reminder of what could befall them if they failed to take possession of God's promise.

With the above in mind, the wilderness sojourn was not without redeeming features, if not for one generation then for the next. Commentators have suggested both religious and social factors. The wilderness has appealed from antiquity to those who want to escape the distractions of secular life and set their attention on the things of God. There is little in the *midbar* to find distracting.

The wilderness experience also has a leveling influence on those who must cooperate in order to survive.

> Here each member is as important as any other, and has the right and opportunity of making his voice felt at the 'assembly'. Within it, to be sure, the elders, who are presumed to have wisdom as well as age, play a dominant role and their opinions carry great weight, particularly since no formal vote is taken, but rather a consensus is reached on issues confronting the group.[17]

We extrapolate from this that chaos encourages people to bond together, and face a corporate challenge. If they fail to do so, they separately succumb. As often observed, united we stand; divided we fall.

Even so, we would not as a rule want to extend the wilderness experience, but endure it by God's grace. Xavier Leon-Defour consequently comments: "This mystique of the flight to the desert has its grandeur, but in the measure in which it would isolate itself from the concrete event in which it originates, it may tend to degenerate into a sterile evasion--God has not called us to live in the desert, but to traverse the desert to live in the promised land."[18]   John the Baptist would come preaching the kingdom of God in the wilderness of Judea. Jesus would be led into the wilderness to be tempted by the devil.   Leon-Defour speculates further: "In a certain sense, it can be said that Christ is our desert--in Him we have overcome the trial, in Him we have perfect communion with God. Henceforth, the desert as place and time is fulfilled in Jesus. Figure gives way to reality."

In the end times, "water will gush forth in the wilderness and streams in the desert" (Isa. 35:7). The *midbar* will thereupon become God's garden, and to the utter amazement of all.

All this lay in the future. For now, the barren wilderness resembled a primordial void. Chaos would prevail but for the grace of God. There was no constructive alternative but to press on in confidence of God's unfailing provision. If one were to falter, death would soon claim its prize.

THE PROMISED LAND

We read that the Hebrews crossed over the Jordan opposite Jericho (Jos. 3:16), some five miles north of the Dead Sea. Beyond *the City of the Palms*, one looks up toward the central hill country, at which point precipitation falls off abruptly toward the eastern approaches. Yohanan Aharoni comments:

> The climate of Palestine is best defined as the outcome of the struggle between these two diversified powers. The westerly winds bring the wet storms of winter and the refreshing summer breezes from the sea, while the easterly winds bring with them the dust and dryness of the desert, hot-burning in summer and cold but dry during the winter.[19]

This meteorological system provided the contrasting imagery of the two ways: that of the wicked and righteous. "The earth dries up and withers" under divine judgement (Isa. 24:4), as if beset by the hot, dry air from out of the wilderness. Nothing can hope to survive for long.

When the heavens withheld their rain, wilderness conditions encroached upon the land. Tribal people from the desert fringe compounded the problem by pillaging the villages. Chaotic conditions would result.

On other occasions, the land welcomed its inhabitants. The ancient Egyptian traveler Sinuhe reported: "Figs were in it, and grapes. It had more wine than water. Plentiful was its honey, abundant its olives. Every kind of fruit was on its trees. Barley was there, and emmer. There was no limit to any kind of cattle." It was not only the land of promise, but a land with promise.

"As the deer pants for streams of water, O God, so my soul pants for you, O God" (Psa. 42:1). Such is the disposition of the righteous, to search out the refreshing streams fed by rain and dew from off the sea. The righteous confess: "The Lord is my shepherd, I shall not be in want.

He makes me lie down in green pastures, he leads me beside quiet waters, he restores my soul" (Psa. 23:1-3).

Care must be taken not to defile the land. Isaiah continues the lament introduced earlier: "The earth is defiled by its people; they have disobeyed the laws, violated the statutes and broken the everlasting covenant. Therefore a curse consumed the earth; the people must bear their guilt" (24:5-6).

The chaos paradigm played to a cosmopolitan audience. Canaan was strategically situated between two great population centers of the ancient world: Egypt and Mesopotamia, where three continents joined. When Israel failed, it was a reminder to the nations of divine justice; when she succeeded, it was indicative of God's blessing.

The prophets did not hesitate to make explicit the chaotic consequences for the nations around them. Isaiah reproached the Egyptians: "The waters of the river will dry up, and the river will be parched and dry. ...Every sown field along the Nile will become parched, will blow away and be no more" (19:5,7). This invoked God's wrath in response to the peoples' wickedness.

As there was cause for concern, so there was reason for hope. *In that day* Egypt will resemble a woman cowering from a threatened blow; *in that day* there will be an altar raised to the Lord on its border; *in that day* they will acknowledge the Lord; *in that day* there will be a highway from Egypt to Assyria. "The Egyptians and Assyrians will worship together. *In that day* Israel will be the third, along with Egypt and Assyria, a blessing on the earth. The Lord Almighty will bless them, saying, 'Blessed by Egypt my people, Assyria my handiwork, and Israel my inheritance'" (Isa. 19:23-25).

The chaos theme was played out in various contexts. First, as mentioned above, with nature. When the scorching winds blow off the desert, chaos extends its grasp. When rain and dew bathes the land, life in all its rich variety springs forth.

Second, in a corporate setting. When the people neglect their covenant, society starts to unravel. The longer they put off a day of reckoning, the worse the situation becomes. When, at last, they repent and return, order returns. They again experience the blessings of God.

Third, in personal terms. Where sin enters, chaos takes hold. Life becomes fragmented and futile. With reconciliation, God picks up the pieces and puts them back together again.

Fourth, embracing the others, in religious context. When we put ourselves first, there is no room for other considerations. When we place

God first, we think of others, and ourselves in relationship to God and others.

Regardless of our response, we cannot alter the conditions. Randomness, as the chaos theorists remind us, occurs within a determined system. A system from Biblical perspective generated by God's sovereignty, expressive of His benevolent purpose, plagued by good gone wrong, and eventually to yield to His righteous resolve.

Within such a system, we may choose. No, we must choose! Procrastination is itself a choice.

We may turn away out of fear of what might befall us. If so, our worst fears become realized. Or we claim God's promises and experience His blessing. If so, every step we take becomes in a manner of speaking holy ground.

All things considered, the author of Hebrews concludes: "Let us, therefore, make every effort to enter that rest, so that no one will fall by following their example of disobedience" (4:11). The promised land still beckons those faced with the chaotic conditions of life.

CHAOTIC TIME OF THE JUDGES

Failure to completely conquer the land and to drive out its inhabitants proved to be Israel's undoing. The Hebrew people became content to settle down, and in many instances intermarry with the idolatrous Canaanites (Judg. 3:5-6). Religious syncretism joined with political compromise to tragically weaken ethnic and religious resolve.

To make things still worse, there was a marked decline in leadership quality with adverse results. There were none even remotely comparable with Moses or his successor Joshua until the Lord raised up Samuel. "The people served the Lord throughout the lifetime of Joshua and of the elders who outlived him and who had seen all the great things the Lord had done for Israel" (2:7). Their faith wavered thereafter, and their fortunes took a turn for the worse. A godly heritage is easily squandered.

The Hebrew tribes became subject to one regional ruler after another. Seeing they would not restrain the sin within, they could not contain the evil without. Illustrative of their dilemma:

> The Israelites did evil in the eyes of the Lord; they forgot the Lord their God and served the Baals and the Asherahs. The anger of the Lord burned against Israel so that he sold them into the hands of Cushan-Rishathaim king of Aram Haharaim, to whom the Israelites were subject for eight years (3:7-8).

They thereupon cried out to the Lord and He raised up for them a deliverer. The spirit of the Lord came upon the appointed one so that he/she was enabled to break the bonds of slavery and usher in a time of peace.

With the passing of time, the people began to neglect their religious and social responsibilities. After which, "once again the Israelites did evil in the eyes of the Lord," and became subject to the Moabite king Eglon.

So matters continued with painful monotony: one cycle followed the previous one. Chaos visited time and again, as an unwelcome and often extended guest. Opportunity gained was readily lost through indifference, indulgence, and indolence..

Even so, one can make out God's benevolent design, primarily with regard to His sovereignty, righteousness, mercy, and the importance of faith. God's *sovereignty* was particularly expressed by means of raising up and enabling the various judges to bring deliverance. It mattered not in the least that the contest was often unequal; one with God was always in the majority.

From chaos perspective, sovereignty seems best understood in dynamic terms. As mentioned in an earlier context, it appears preeminently as a *resolve* that persists until successful. The kingdom of God is as it operates.

God's *righteousness* can be seen in His allowing the people to experience the bitter fruit of their evil behavior. He did not shelter them from self-inflicted torment.

God decidedly does not bend the rules. He does what is right under all conditions. He never wavers from His righteous ways.

His *mercy* was revealed in repeatedly heeding the petitions of a recalcitrant people. Each time they call out to Him, regardless of their former unfaithfulness, He responds with a deliverer and an interim of peace. His hand remained extended.

God also knows when His mercy will no longer serve any good purpose. Our time will eventually run out. We presume at our own risk.

Even though we do not discover much in the way of moral grandeur in the judges to inspire us, we should be impressed by their *faith*. Hebrews expounds in like manner: "I do not have time to tell about Gideon, Barak, Sampson, Jephthah...who through faith conquered kingdoms, administered justice, and gained what was promised" (11:32-33).

The righteous shall live by faith: faith in God, faith in His direction, faith in His provision, and faith in His endurance. Let God be true, and all others false. Never doubt His word.

Seek His guidance. Follow it once found. Let nothing and no one dissuade you. You will not be disappointed.

Trust His enablement. Whatever God would have us do, He will provide the means. It is not for lack of provision but availability that we often fail.

Have confidence in His faithfulness. He specializes in finishing what He begins. As sometimes put, work as if all depends on you, but trust as though all depends on God.

We cannot ever be certain just how things will work out, any more than we can predict the precise set in chaos theory. Each situation requires an unique approach, but God is eminently creative. So are we reminded from a troubled period when there was no continuity in leadership, and *everyone did as he saw fit* (21:25).

The author obviously anticipates a more favorable alternative. The time will come when magistrates will govern justly, employing their God-given talents for His glory and the people's benefit. When such time comes, order will in large measure displace chaos. Any government (worthy of that ascription) should be thought of as better than none.

Even so, we need bear in mind that systems need maintenance. If not, chaos returns. When it does, the result may be worse than first experienced.

With such in mind, remember the turbulent time of the judges. Recall how the people got into trouble by neglecting their covenant obligation, how painful was their experience as a result, how deliverance came about, and what blessings followed in its wake. Then, as the saying goes, may the wind be to your back.

MAKING OF THE MONARCHY

While the people prospered under Samuel's wise leadership, his sons did not share his sterling character. In addition, the Philistines in particular constituted an ever present threat. When the Hebrew people decided that they could wait no longer, they demanded a king *such as all the other nations have* (1 Sam. 8:5).

Kingship is an old and well-established phenomenon in Israel's international context, but is new, problematic, and dangerous for Israel. Early Israel had emerged as a subversive alternative to human leadership. Now the question of monarchy has surfaced again in Israel with fresh vitality and insistence as thought the old painful memory of Pharaoh no longer exists.[20]

There was more to the demand than would meet the eye.

Their motive was to conform to the world about them rather than to abide by the holy and perfect constitution that God had given them under Moses in the form of the Pentateuchal codes. There was a definite sense in which they were setting aside the laws of God as inadequate for their needs and falling into step with the idolatrous heathen.[21]

The making of the monarchy reminds us how fragile our social institutions: how vulnerable to the erosion of time or some sudden crisis. We need to build with care, and never take our heritage for granted. Chaos plagues our every effort.

With the rise of the monarchy, the king became the dominant unifying figure. He was not simply the ruler, but along with the people subject to their covenant obligations. He could not, any more than they, make arbitrary decisions based on special privilege.

A classic case in point finds Nathan confronting David concerning his adultery with Bathsheba (2 Sam. 12). "There were two men in a certain town," the prophet began. One was very rich with many sheep and cattle, latter provided nothing from his bounty, but seized the poor man's lamb to provide hospitality.

"As surely as the Lord lives," David broke in, "the man who did this deserves to die!" Whereupon, Nathan solemnly replied: "You are the man!" After the prophet had further admonished him, the king concluded: "I have sinned against the Lord!" His royal position provided him no immunity.

The *will of the people* was much more than a literary metaphor in monarchial times. It implied the consent to be governed, the willingness to cooperate, and the possibility that allegiance might shift. Drawing from a common covenant tradition, the people were individually and corporately responsible to God and for one another.

The dynastic economy moreover created the need for an intricate system of checks and balances. Most prominent in the dynastic mix were the prophets. "From the time of your forefathers left Egypt until now, day after day, again and again I sent my servants the prophets," God reminded His people (Jer. 7:25). While the prophetic office did not originate with the monarchy, it came to act as a religious conscience and balance off the political bureaucracy.

The prophets exhibited a keen sensitivity to evil, coupled with an unrelenting commitment to the covenant agenda. Where to us a matter like cheating might be considered of minor consequence, to the prophet it was a serious offence; where to us exploitation of the poor might appear regrettable, to the prophet it was an affront to the Almighty; where to us marital unfaithfulness might treated as less than ideal, it was for the prophet a disaster of major proportions. They could sense the approach of chaos when oblivious to others. They also strove to fine-tune the monarchy to its covenant stipulations. "Seek the Lord while he may be found, call on him while he is near. Let the wicked forsake his way and the evil man his thoughts. Let him turn to the Lord, and he will have mercy on him, and to our God for he will freely pardon" (Isa. 55:6-7).

The priests along with their cult practices were another important ingredient in the dynastic system of checks and balances. They were not an auxiliary to but at the heart of Hebrew life and devotion.

The central sanctuary was of critical importance to sustaining the monarchy. The people were told to bring their offerings to Jerusalem rather than raise altars more convenient for their purposes. Josiah received lavish praise for razing competitive altars among his other reforms: "Neither before nor after Josiah was there a king like him who turned to the Lord as he did--with all his heart and with all his soul and reforms: "Neither before nor after Josiah was there a king like him who turned to the Lord as he did--with all his heart and with all his soul and with all his strength, in accordance with all the Law of Moses" (2 Kings 23:25).

Not to be overlooked in the dynastic mix, the Hebrew sage often played a decisive role. He may actually have been the most pervasive and constant contributor to the monarchy of the special cases we have considered. He was part of the general weave of monarchial times, everywhere assumed and highly regarded.

In all probability, sages provided an advisory role in the royal court, as was customary in antiquity. This would account for Sennacherib's field commander urging Hezekiah not to rely on those giving him counsel (Isa. 36:4-7). They were likely also responsible for compiling the proverbs of Solomon (Prov. 25:1).

The best monarchial scenario consisted of all aspects of the dynastic mix working together to further God's purposes; the worst was a contagion starting at any point and impacting on the rest. Three generations from Saul to Solomon cover only about a century, but witnessed the rapid expansion and defects of a fledgling kingdom. All three of Israel's kings began well, but ended tragically.

> Saul's disobedience, David's sin in the matter of Bath-Sheba and Uriah, and Solomon's idolatry left their mark upon kings and people. The nation was not without a prophetic voice to call for repentance and trust in Israel's God, but Israel's political success had within it the germs of failure. With the death of Solomon the kingdom was shattered, never to be united again.[22]

As concerns *systems' maintenance*, the making of the monarchy provides a striking case in point. What transpired warns us to plan wisely. While the people had legitimate concerns (with a crisis in leadership and threat from without), they had not calculated the implications of their request (as an affront to God) or the high cost to themselves. Sometimes our remedies prove worse than what ails us in the first place.

Of no less importance, we need to execute effectively. With such erstwhile friends as chronicled in Scripture, God needs no enemies. Bungling saints create more than their share of problems.

Once under way, we should watch for signs of turbulence in the system. Soon it will be too late to correct the operation. If we act preemptively, we may alleviate the difficulty.

We also must learn to accept the wise counsel of others. Had the

Hebrew rulers been disposed to listen to the warning of the prophets, all would have been spared a great deal of suffering. Turning a deaf ear, they turned their people toward captivity.

Covenant or chaos: these appear as the options confronting the monarchy. If faithful to the covenant, the people would dwell safely in the land. If not, chaos would return as a sword in the hand of an alien military commander.

TALE OF TWO KINGDOMS

When Rehoboam had ascended to the throne, the people petitioned him: "Your father put a heavy yoke on us, but now lighten the harsh labor and the heavy yoke he put on us, and we will serve you" (1 Kings 12:4). When he refused to grant their wishes, the northern tribes revolted under Jeroboam.

Jeroboam set up rival sanctuaries in Bethel and Dan, erected golden calves, and consecrated priests regardless of lineage. He blatantly chose political expedience over covenant obligations. The course of the Northern Kingdom was set in cement.

The prophets attempted to intervene. Isaiah declared God's awesome holiness, man's sinfulness before Him, and the opportunity for healing (cf. 6:1-7). When his pleas went unheeded, the prophet increasingly turned his attention to the anticipated Messiah, a believing remnant, and consummation with *the things to come* (41:22). The Messiah (anointed) would serve as had Moses to deliver the people from oppression; a faithful remnant would respond to God's initiative; all this would take place in a future time set off from the present course of events.

By the time Hosea had assumed rule, his options were severely limited. He was vassal a of Assyria. Awaiting dynastic succession, he appealed to Egypt for help and discontinued his tribute to Assyria. Three years later (722 B.C.) Samaria lay in ruins.

Massive relocation followed. Israelites were removed to Persia; their place taken immigrants from Babylonia, Elam, and Syria. Thus came to pass Amos' dire prediction: "For I will give the command, and I will shake the house of Israel among all the nations as grain is shaken in a sieve, and not a pebble will reach to the ground" (9:9).

"The Southern Kingdom, meanwhile, did show some sense of national destiny, epitomized in an idealized image of David. Every Judahite king was a direct descendant of this king and aimed to perpetuate his image."[23] The Southern Kingdom had been more responsive to the message of the prophets, which in turn, increased its *scope* of possibilities (as documented in chaos theory). This made possible the revival under Josiah and the wholesome rule of Hezekiah.

Some insisted on blaming their predecessors for their troubles. They would glibly repeat the proverb: "The fathers eat sour grapes, and the children's teeth are set on edge" (Ezek. 18:2). It was a part truth at best. While impacted by others, we do not have to compound the problem and may contribute to its resolution.

Time was nevertheless running out. "My people have committed two sins: they have forsaken me, the spring of living water, and have dug their own cisterns, broken cisterns that cannot hold waster" (Jer. 2:13). They had spurned God's covenant grace in favor of their own paltry works. They resembled cracked cisterns, unable to retain the water of life.

The unthinkable eventually came to pass: Jerusalem, city of the Great King, lay in ruins. Perhaps a third of the people were either taken into captivity or fled to Egypt for refuge. Only certain of the common people were left behind. Devastation was everywhere. Life was in turmoil.

This brings to mind Koplan and Glass' definition of chaos as "operiodic (never repeated) bounded dynamics in a deterministic system with sensitive dependence on initial conditions."[24] The term *strange attractor* recurs in chaos theory to express the convergence of events toward initial conditions in a bounded (finite) system. It is deemed *strange* in that the precise events are unpredictable. As illustrated with the tale of two kingdoms, the bounded dynamics of each kingdom differed from one another, and in each successive step within itself. As characterized earlier, the northern kingdom went into a tight spiral from which there was no recovery. In contrast, the southern kingdom waxed and waned until at last it succumbed to the evil that threatened its survival.

What the two kingdoms shared in common was a sensitive dependence on initial conditions. Jeroboam erected altars of convenience for the people to worship, so that they need not travel to Jerusalem. This introduced idolatry and led to the downfall of the kingdom. Rehoboam, contrasted favorable by the Biblical writer, reigned seventeen years in Jerusalem, "the city the Lord had chosen out of all the tribes of Israel in which to put his Name" (1 Kings 14:21). He demonstrated in this manner his obedience to God, and encouraged others to do so.

Chaos theory refers to behavioral repetition as *iteration*. It creates a dynamic system in which some things appear predictable and others not. One could imagine that the northern kingdom was asking for trouble, but not the precise events which would transpire. We would expect something better from the southern kingdom, but without precision or sense of limitation.

Jeremiah portrayed God as actively engaged in tearing down and rebuilding, drawing from the analogy of a potter recasting his clay (18:12-17). As the potter proceeded, some defect might arise, causing him to recast the clay and start over. It would appear for the moment that his purpose had been frustrated, only to be realized in a new vessel.

The prophet was taken with the potter's skill in turning seeming failure into resounding success. One would expect no less from God. As dark as the tunnel might at the moment appear, there was always a glimmer of light at its end.

TRAUMA OF EXILE

"By the rivers of Babylon we sat and wept when we remembered Zion" (Psa. 137:1). "Sing us one of the songs of Zion!" urged *our tormentors*, but "how can we sing the songs of the Lord in a foreign land?"

The exile was a disaster of major proportions: politically, economically, socially, and most critical--religiously. How were the people to explain the demise of the Davidic Dynasty with which Yahweh's sovereign reign had become associated, the temple where His worship was carried out, and His chosen people separated from the land of promise? "In short, almost all the old symbol systems had been rendered useless. Almost all of the old institutions no longer functioned."[25] Consider the loss of the temple in particular. It was regarded both as a miniature of the world and its center (the navel of the earth).

> The welfare of Israel, nay, of the whole world of seventy nations, was dependent on the proper performance of the service in the Temple, each state and each moment of which had a closely determined effect on some corresponding stage or moment in the beneficial working of the forces of nature.[26]

Thereby all that seemingly stood between an ordered society and chaos was the temple ritual.

With the temple in ruins, one might suppose that the crops would begin to fail, the political structures come crashing down, and society loose any sense of cohesion. All this seemed to be coming to pass. It was a worst case scenario.

The problem persisted on a theoretical and practical level. As a *theoretical* consequence, how were they to explain the disaster befalling God's chosen people? The prophets had primed them to acknowledge responsibility for the events which came to pass. While this rationale helped them get through the initial shock and cultivated a more contrite spirit, it also had its limits. The severity of the situation coupled with its protracted character encouraged the people to look elsewhere, not for an alternative explanation but a more comprehensive one.

Micah had suggested a larger purpose for Israel's suffering: "Therefore Israel will be abandoned until the time when she who is in labor gives birth and the rest of his brothers return to join the Israelites" (5:3). The people took this to mean that they were experiencing messianic travail, signifying that they must persevere in anticipation of the joy to be realized with birth of the messianic era. Indeed, they had sinned and deserved to be chastised, but God would bring good out of an exceedingly desperate situation--for themselves and all nations.

As a *practical* consideration, the problem of pain can be variously managed. Here it is portrayed as a facet of a larger, benevolent purpose. If one suffers, count it a privilege for contributing to the greater good.

Thus were the Hebrew people able to maintain their credibility as a chosen people. No matter how dismal the prospect, there was always a light at the end of the tunnel. As for the interim, God would sustain and cause them to be a blessing to others. Such hope lent dignity to a subjugated people. They could stand tall when required to bow low.

The Hebrew hope was enlarged, projected, and expressed in terms of a remnant as the result of the exile. It was *enlarged* to view the experience of Israel in connection with universal history. This was not strictly speaking a new development since God was understood as sovereign, and had explicitly promised to bless the nations through His chosen people. Even so, their attention had become increasingly focused on their own affairs, until forced to broaden their horizons in a foreign land among Gentile people.

This seems to have intensified tension between two Hebrew ideals: as concerns Israel as a holy (separate) people, and as a light to the nations. It seems difficult to have it both ways. It suggests perhaps a worldly holiness, what some characterize as being in but not of the world.

Its hope was also *projected* to the future. During the more encouraging times, it might have appeared that God's promises were on the verge of being fulfilled. It now seemed clear: the people had expected too much, too soon. Wisdom cautioned patience and piety accepted its counsel.

Still, it must have seemed as if God was dragging His feet. How long will You allow the evil to prosper? When will You deliver the righteous from their suffering? How long?

Its hope was finally expressed in connection with a *faithful remnant.* Daniel and his companions represented such a remnant. They observed their dietary regulations and stated time of prayer in spite of the threat of death. Standing firm in the face of adversity, they could count of God's present enablement and subsequent reward.

Many fell by the wayside. They succumbed to religious syncretism, social pressures, and/or personal advancement. There remained only the faithful few. Broad was the way that led to destruction, and many accommodated themselves to it; narrow was the way to life, and few had courage to travel it.

Qualifications aside, the pattern remained constant. Order gave way to chaos, and chaos to order, as if by design. Welcome to the real world!

CONSTRUCTIVE APPROACH TO CHAOS

"We generally treat the Book of Job as a commentary on suffering, but is much more than that. Pain certainly rushes to the forefront (both as physical affliction and mental anguish), but wisdom is the more persisting subject."[27] The Job narrative counsels us on how to live in God's world, and by His grace. It is as such a timeless treatise on living with chaos.

Job was a good man, who feared God and shunned evil. He had a large family and many possessions. The patriarch had in fact no peer "among all the people of the East" (1:3).

Then his world began to come apart with dramatic suddenness. A messenger brought word that the Sabeans had attacked and carried off his oxen and donkeys, and put his servants to the sword. *While he was still speaking* another arrived with the report that fire had fallen from heaven burning up his sheep and servants; *while he was still speaking* still another announced that three Chaldean raiding parties had driven off his camels; *while he was still speaking* a final messenger informed him that a mighty wind had collapsed the house where his children were eating and all were dead.

Job's first reaction was to rend his garment and shave his head, as signs of mourning. "Naked I came from my mother's womb, and naked I will depart. The Lord gave and the Lord has taken away; may the Lord be praised" (1:21). "Job feels himself now already as good a dead; stripped naked of his possessions, he is as if he were already prepared for burial."[28] The narrator comments on the patriarch's pious response: "In all this, Job did not sin by charging God with wrongdoing."

We have an advantage over Job in being made privy to an interchange between God and Satan. "Does Job fear God for nothing?" the latter impugned. "Have you not put a hedge around him and his household and everything he has? ...But stretch out your hand and strike everything he has, and he will surely curse you to your face." God thereupon allowed the patriarch to be tested, in order to demonstrate that his trust was in God rather than circumstances.

Satan was not convinced: "Skin for skin!" (2:4). "A man will give all he has for his own life. But stretch out your hand and strike his flesh and bones, and he will surely curse you to your face."

With the triad of God, Satan, and Job alerts us to the nonlinear (complex) character of life. As a result, there can be no simple correlation between behavior and recompense; no more than we can chart the course of the earth simply on its attraction to the sun.

Ivars Peterson elaborates on the latter phenomenon: "The competing tugs of these celestial compatriots (planets within our solar system) append a restless spectrum to minute wiggles to a basic, sun-dominated motion, causing a jangle of deviations from perfect geometry." Not this alone, but "even the imperceptible, evanescent whispers of the lesser objects in the solar systems--asteroids, satellites, and comets--add to the celestial chorus, as does the thrum of the fluttering solar wind of accelerated particles and radiation continually erupting from the sun." Not only these, but at the same time the globe on which we live and spins on its own axis even as it orbits the sun.

> Like a gargantuan twirling top, it wobbles and tilts. It shudders with every earthquake and twists fitfully with every giant swirl within its atmosphere or sea. Any unevenness in its shape or in the materials making up its crust unbalances its movement and provides a lever by which the sun and other bodies can further wrench Earth from a pure and simple motion.[29]

Job seems to sense something of this complex character of life as related to his situation. In contrast, his associates seem quite oblivious to it. They suppose that there is a linear (simple) correlation between behavior and recompense.

The test enters its second phase with the affliction of Job himself. While such information as we have does not allow a certain diagnosis, Job suffers from a severe skin disorder, resulting in inflamation, blisters, giving off an offensive order, and intense itching. He removes himself to a heap of dung ashes to scrape away at his festering flesh with a potsherd.

Job nevertheless remained resolute. "Shall we accept good from God, and not trouble?" Several thousand words later, the patriarch was again commended--faults notwithstanding. After which, we read that the "Lord blessed the latter part of Job's life more than the first" (42:12).

How are we to deal constructively with chaos? Job's response seems to offer several suggestions. *First, recognize all of life as being within God's benevolent purpose.* Paul confidently asserted: "We know that in all things God works for the good of those who love him, who have been called according to his purpose" (Rom. 8:28). Whether apostle or patriarch, they experienced what C.S. Lewis referred to as *God exploiting evil for good.*

The text of Job serves as a prime example. It has been a means of bringing comfort and instruction, from generation to generation, to a multitude of readers. His pain has been our gain.

Second, *be reminded of the essential character of life in God's world.*

> All situations can be opportunities for us to foster a deeper communion with the Almighty, minister to and be ministered to by others, and accept our responsibility for the world about us. Those unenviable situations are not only included but may be the better instances for grasping the true significance of life and making progress in our spiritual pilgrimage.[30]

Here superficialities are stripped away, and we get down to essential issues.

Evil may be less our undoing than the trivial. We major on minor concerns and minor on major ones. It is as if we had turned life upside down, and need to turn it right-side up.

Third, benefit from tradition without being enslaved by it. Bildad invited Job: "Ask the former generations and find out what their fathers learned" (8:8). As for us, "we were born only yesterday and know nothing, and our days on earth are but a shadow." Even so, we ought not accept tradition uncritically, or think it a simple matter to apply to current circumstances.

Learn from the past; live in the present; live toward the future. Such would seem the patriarch's sage advice. Conversely, some would live in the past, neglect the present, and ignore the future.

Fourth, *cultivate faith without allowing it to degenerate into credulity.* "We all have believed something that we no longer hold. Some beliefs strain under the weight of contrary evidence until they collapse. Others seem to be refined in the crucible of life until they become strong and durable."[31] Job's beliefs were of the latter sort. They were in the end vindicated.

In another context, I reasoned: "We do not have the choice between faith and unbelief. We can only choose between rival faiths. Such arguments as may be leveled against faith, as such, cut all ways. We are all entered on the same course: to discover a credible faith."[32]

Finally, *accept circumstances as the means through which God may express His grace.* A chaplain was called upon to minister to those who had survived conflict physically or emotionally impaired. It was not until they could accept their handicap that progress began to take place. Like Job, they symbolically shed their ashes to cooperate with God and vigorously renew life.

C.S. Lewis thought that we cooperate with God in rectifying the suffering around us through two primary means: accepting circumstances as God's means for good, and repenting of evil. The former encompasses natural evil, and the latter focuses on moral evil.

The Job analogue served not only to guide godly individuals but corporate Israel. The Hebrew people thought themselves blessed beyond all other nations, only to fall on dismal days. They hoped that God would restore them to a more glorious future than the past. In anticipation the devout would respond: "Blessed be He!"

SILENCE OF GOD

Babylon did not have long to gloat over its hapless Hebrew captives. Within a half century the once mighty power had capitulated. Cyrus was enthusiastically welcomed to deliver a weary people from an unpopular regime. He issued a decree during his first year of reign authorizing the rebuilding of the temple at Jerusalem and return of the sacred vessels for use therein.

However promising the edict may have appeared, the years ahead would be filled with disillusionment, disappointment, and discouragement. The people had anticipated that their return would usher in a golden age. They would experience *shalom* (peace/well-being). Jerusalem would come to be the center for universal worship.

Their experience was quite the opposite. The returning remnant faced hostility from those living in the land. The nations seemed unconcerned. Disillusionment set in.

Disappointment followed on the heals of disillusionment. The people had counted on much, but had to settle for little. It was a bitter pill to swallow.

Discouragement rounded out the triad. Zeal languished. The work of rebuilding faltered. Jerusalem remained largely in ruin seventy-five years after the edict of restoration. The people struggled through poor growing seasons and partial crop failure. Perhaps most disconcerting, the spring of the prophets ran dry. "Silence would then be the symbol of destruction and the word that of redemption."[33]

The people were forced to put up with the silence of God, without any relief in sight. It continued until it seemed deafening to the pious. As for the others, it allowed them to continue in their perverse ways without reprimand.

The silent years, between the testaments, were not uneventful. Philip of Macedon took the initial step toward forming the Hellenic League as rival to Persia. When Philip was murdered in 336 B.C., his mantle fell upon his youthful son Alexander. The latter, tutored by Aristotle, became an ardent exporter of Hellenic culture.

Hellenism played to mixed Jewish reviews. Some saw it as a serious threat to cherished traditions; others thought it a means to break out of inhibiting ethnic restrictions.

Matters came to a head with the Seleucid ruler Antiochus IV, who determined to Hellenize Jerusalem and its surrounding area by force. "Greek soldiers and their paramours performed licentious heathen rites in the very Temple courts. Swine were sacrificed on the altar. The drunken orgy associated with the worship of Bachus was made compulsory."[34] On the other hand, Jews were forbidden to practice circumcision, Sabbath observance, and their liturgical calendar. Copies of the Scripture were ordered destroyed.

The Maccabean revolt was soon kindled. The Seleucids failed first to take the rag-tag revolutionaries seriously enough, and were afterward distracted by insurrection at home. The Jews were consequently granted control over their internal affairs.

"In Palestine the strength--both moral and physical--of the Maccabees was fast waning. The news of the chaos in Palestine reached Rome. Pompey, the Roman general who had been so successful in bringing Roman power to the East, determined to intervene."[35] Josephus succinctly concluded that "Judea was made tributary to the Romans."

The prophetic silence recalled the silence of primordial times, when the earth was formless and empty, before God uttered His eight creative mandates. It was as if the pages were turned back to a time when the earth was inhospitable to life.

Even so, they could expect that God would break His silence. "See, I send you the prophet Elijah before the great and dreadful day of the Lord comes. He will turn the hearts of the fathers to their children, and the children to their father; or else I will come and strike the land with a curse" (Mal. 4:6).

The ministry of the coming prophet was described as if

bridging the generation gap. The fifth commandment implies that the home was essentially the school of the community. There, in a 'world in miniature', authority and submission, love and loyalty, obedience and trust could learned as nowhere else, and, with the word of God as guide in the home, society could be changed.[36]

The alternative was that they would reject the words of this latter-day prophet, and the land would be cursed.

As for the interim, learn to trust your ways to God. Obey His will as previously revealed, and wait on subsequent instruction. It is not as a rule for lack of information that we fail, but for failing to act on the information we have.

In any case, life goes on. As sometimes put, to live is to change. Conversely, dig in only in anticipation of death. So it would seem in prophetic perspective, and with this chaos theory take no exception.

THE FUTURE NOW

We have with the advent of Christ reached a critical juncture with the Biblical narrative in chaos perspective. It seems best to understand this in two connections: with *a basin of attraction* and *bifurcation*. "A basin of attraction of an attracting set is the set of all the initial conditions in the phase space whose trajectories go to that attracting set."[37] That is, the basin contains the variables within the initial conditions.

One of the variables in some sense present in the initial conditions was God's intent to send the Messiah in the fullness of time. Scripture manifestly does not represent this as an afterthought.

The term *bifurcation* refers to a sudden qualitative change in the nature of a solution, as when the parameters are changed. Such was the case with the advent of Christ, and the shift from the present age to the inauguration of the age to come. It was not simply more of the same (quantitative), but something novel and promising.

The event was marked by a seemingly insignificant development: the birth of a child in a manger. There were however intimations that this would be of profound significance. Such as we observe with the announcement to Mary, comments by others, the birth of John the Baptist, and the visit of the wise men.

Moreover, we have discovered from chaos perspective that an apparently small change at a crucial point can create changes of a major proportion. As when some modest shift in weather conditions builds into a storm of dramatic proportions. We noted this phenomenon earlier with Adam's defection, and pick it up again with the events to follow.

In brief, they relate to an itinerant rabbi from an inconspicuous village in Galilee, who was put to death as a trouble-maker. This might have passed with little notice, but was not meant to be. This one solitary life would impact on mankind as none before or after.

At the synagogue in Nazareth and after reading from Isaiah, Jesus declared: "Today this scripture is fulfilled in your hearing" (Luke 4:20).

Everything previous could be understood henceforth as promise; everything including the present as fulfillment.

Thus are we reminded that Jesus takes center stage concerning personal salvation, redemptive history, and the restoration of nature. Jesus is the center as concerns *personal salvation.* Peter resolutely insisted: "Salvation is found in on one else, for there is no other name under heaven given to me by which we must be saved" (Acts 4:12).

The setting for the apostle's cryptic witness is as follows. He had healed a crippled beggar, causing quite a stir among the people. When he and John continued to preach to the people, the religious leaders took them to task. "By what power or what name did you do this?" they demanded. At which, Peter responded as noted above. The physical miracle invokes a spiritual reality.

Jesus is also center as concerns *redemptive history.* The author of Hebrews writes: "In the past God spoke to our forefathers through the prophets at many times and in various ways, but in these last days he has spoken to us by his Son" (1:1-2). God had spoken previously, in one context or another. Now He speaks *in these last days*, as a climax to what proceeded it. .

The B.C./A.D. dichotomy is a vivid reminder of Jesus' centrality. The point is obscured by the innocuous reference to the *common era.* The latter serves more as a concession to those who see matters differently.

Jesus is finally the center as concerns *the restoration of nature.* His nature miracles, such as His stilling of the storm, may be viewed as tokens of things to come. Paul confidently concludes: "For the creation was subjected to frustration, not by its own choice, but by the will of the one who subjected it, in hope that the creation itself will be liberated from its bondage to decay and brought into the glorious freedom of the children of God" (Rom. 8:20-21).

The apostle views the creation and heirs-by-faith bonded together in suffering and hope. They experience the pain of child-birth, until the time of delivery. They wait patiently but in steadfast hope for the consummation in Christ.

Jesus is not only the center in the ways described above, but also alters the parameters of life. "No one sews a patch of unshrunk cloth on an old garment," Jesus cautioned, "for the patch will pull away from the garment, making the tear worse" (Matt. 9:16). Nor does one pour new wine into old wineskins. Nor should one suppose that new could be contained within the old dispensation.

Christ is not only there at the center, and with the setting of new parameters, but there for us. "For God did not send his Son into the world to condemn the world, but to save the world through him" (John 1:17). He remains for us even when we are not for ourselves.

The implications are far reaching. God has established a beachhead on enemy soil. He will not allow His forces to be driven back into the sea. Final victory is altogether assured.

Paul rhetorically inquires: "Who shall separate us from the love of Christ? Shall trouble or hardship or persecution or famine or nakedness or danger or sword?" (Rom. 8:35). "No, in all these things we are more than conquerors through him who loved us."

"The Spirit himself testifies with our spirit that we are God's children. Now if we are children, then we are heirs--heirs of God and co-heirs with Christ, if indeed we share in his sufferings in order that we may also share in his glory" (Rom. 8:16-17). The apostle elsewhere elaborates: "Though outwardly we are wasting away, yet inwardly we are being renewed day by day" (2 Cor. 4:16).

F.F. Bruce aptly concludes "that the very afflictions and privations which wear down the 'outer nature' are the means used by the Spirit of God to renew the inner being more and more, until at the last the outer nature disappears altogether and the inner being is fully formed after the image of Christ."[38] He who has begun a good work will complete it, to the inestimable benefit of those who trust their way to Him--since the future is now with Christ is the center and circumference of life..

This is the *really real*, as Francis Schaeffer would enthusiastically exclaim. Jesus came into the real world, to combat actual forces, and redeem genuine persons. The gospel has an earthy character. As such, it is emphatically not religious fantasy. The early disciples did not create the events they report, but bore witness to them. They depict the advent narratives as God's initiative. They are secular events with sacred significance.

One would have been hard pressed to predict what was to happen from that moment on. The prophetic scriptures offered some direction, but often appeared enigmatic. Even with the passing of time, the disciples sometimes appear confused. As for the rest, they were attracted and/or offended, often for reasons they hardly understood.

This was not the end, but the beginning of the end. The quiet years would follow, after that Jesus' public ministry, and finally His passion. Then, when the story seemed told, there was a report of His resurrection, and with it of triumphant hope for others.

MASTER OF CHAOS

If I were to choose one pericope to characterized Jesus' public ministry from chaos perspective, it would be His stilling of the storm (Mark. 4:35-41). It was evening when Jesus suggested to His disciples that they go over to the other side of the Sea of Galilee. As they made their way, a violent storm arose, threatening to swamp the boat.

Jesus was asleep in the stern. His disciples awoke Him with the complaint: "Teacher, don't you care if we drown?" Jesus stood to His feet, and rebuked the wind and the waves. Then the wind died down, and the water was calm.

He turned to His disciples, and said to them: "Why are you so afraid? Do you still have no faith?" They were terrified and asked each other: "Who is this? Even the wind and the waves obey him!"

This pericope occurs at a transition in the narrative. Mark has been recounting kingdom parables, and her introduces Jesus authority over nature, the demonic, and death. The waters and death (as previously mentioned) represent chaos, as might the demonic. Each individually or in some combination threaten our survival, and all yield at Christ's rebuke.

Chaos greets us on every hand. We experience it in illness, impotency, inhospitality, natural calamities, social upheavals, or the loss of loved ones. Life always seems to be slipping through our fingers, until there is nothing left.

Such was the world into which Jesus came to minister. Unrolling the Isaiah scroll, He read: "The Spirit of the Lord is on me, because he has anointed me to preach good news to the poor. He has sent me to proclaim freedom for the prisoners and recovery of sight for the blind, to release the oppressed, to proclaim the year of the Lord's favor" (Luke 4:18-19; cf. Isa. 61:1-2). As the eyes of everyone was fixed on Him, Jesus confidently announced: "Today this scripture is fulfilled in your hearing."

Jesus characterized His ministry as good news for the oppressed. *The poor* represent "not only the economically impoverished but all those who

are marginal or excluded from human fellowship, the outcast."[39] Some
are less able to cope with the exigencies of life: those without financial
means, prisoners, blind, and downtrodden. Unable to manage on their
own, they often lack an advocate.

The Master came to ease the burden of the common person, of whom
there were many. He ministered as would a physician to the sick, a
mentor to the uninformed, a consoler to the bereaved. He was as
sometimes characterized *the man devoted to others*. While not an
exclusive designation, it underscores an important feature. His was
essentially a religious message, with profound social and personal
implications. He came preaching that the kingdom of God was near (cf.
Mark 1:15). R. Alan Cole elaborates:

> The news which Jesus now heralded in Galilee was that God's hour had
> struck, the time to which all the Old Testament had looked forward. God's
> reign upon earth, a concept familiar from the prophets, was about to begin (*is
> at hand*). All were therefore called to a change of heart (*repent*) and to a
> belief in this good news.[40]

Cole adds by way of reflection:

> What all had yet to learn, and what proved to be the hardest lesson for the
> disciples of Jesus to learn, was that the reign of God was not (presently) to
> be a sufficient explanation of his sense of separation. Such separation be a
> cataclysmic external triumph in the here and now by an earthly Messiah, but
> a peaceful rule over the hearts of those who responded to the Message.

These may be understood from chaos perspective as *fractals*, since
fractals "have a curious mathematical property: they have essentially the
same structure on all scales."[41]

Taking Jesus' invitation to return to a sacred agenda seriously, we must
be made aware of what Helmut Thielicke refers to as the *sinister
possibilities* of the secular. He expounds:

> With the progress of secularization the world has been able to cease its
> chafing under the yoke of commandments and the strait jacket of so-called
> 'Christian' states and customs. It has been able to organize and constitute
> itself exclusively on the basis of factors already inherent within itself. As a
> result, we have for the first time to see clearly what the world really is.[42]

Granted, the sinister possibilities have not been fully unleashed, but we can see more clearly than anytime since the first century the monstrous potential for chaotic upheaval in a culture which declares its autonomy from God.

Jesus approaches chaos in a preemptive fashion, so as to establish His credentials as Messiah and thereby provide an earnest for the future. Even the winds and waves were said to obey Him; even the power of death had no final control over Him.

Any detailed system of ethics based on Jesus' teaching seems problematic. We are strictly speaking called not to follow His teaching (although we are to observe it); we are mandated to follow Him! We should be prepared to surrender everything held dear in order to be His disciple (cf. Luke 14:33). We must be willing to embrace ridicule, hardship, persecution, and even death. We must not under any circumstances turn back once having taken on the yoke of discipleship.[43]

Jesus lived out the admonition to love others as oneself. He promoted the great prophetic principles of justice, mercy, and the cultivation of peace (well-being). He reminded persons of their social obligations, and the importance of their social institutions. His ministry collides with various forms of current individualism, in keeping with the Hebrew concept of corporate life.

The Master nonetheless maintained a needed balance between corporate and individual concerns. He was always aware of the individual seemingly eclipsed by the crowd. One could not really love others as enjoined, unless he or she had a high regard for self. Society was meant to enhance and enrich the person.

The disciples derive their righteousness vicariously, through Christ who has met the conditions of an acceptable sacrifice. They also encounter chaos vicariously: nothing impacts them that He does not mediate, and no response is apart from His intercession. Christ's chaos formula takes us beyond being *for* us to being *in* and *through* us. Jesus did not so much terminate His public ministry as to extend it through others. As concerns His disciples, it calls less for nostalgic recollection than wholehearted involvement.

Jesus did not eliminate chaos. He restrained it, and in so doing, anticipated a final deliverance. Jesus' live and ministry resembled an earnest for the future. In this sense the kingdom was already present in fractal fashion: small in scale but true to character.

Barry Parker comments as follows: "A good example of a fractal...is an ocean coastline. If you look at it from an airplane, it is jogged, with many inlets and peninsulas. If you look at a small selection of it closer, you see the same structure."[44]   Whether viewed from near or far, the kingdom reveals a striking similarity.

ONCE FOR ALL

Traditional religions not uncommonly provide a sacrificial means to recover the world from chaos. My Nigerian students excitedly shared with me one such occasion. It seemed that an expatriate, unfamiliar with the local customs, broke a taboo by killing a certain reptile. This was thought to have upset the delicate harmony (order) of the universe. Sacrifice was called for. All were called upon to participate regardless of religious persuasion.

Only one elderly man refused. It seemed to him unnecessary to perpetuate sacrifices of any sort, seeing that Jesus had died *once for all*. He remained adamant, even when other Christians compromised to traditional practice and under dire threats from the village folk.

Hebrews concludes: "But now he has appeared once for all at the end of the ages to do away with sin by the sacrifice of himself" (9:26). "The Levitical high priest year after year entered the inner sanctuary. By contrast, Christ's appearance is a single occurrence--it happened once for all. He entered heaven once, that is, at the time of his ascension. The effect of this single appearance lasts forever."[45] Having completed His mission, Christ "sat down on the right hand of God" (10:12).

It bears repetition: "In the past God spoke to our forefathers through the prophets at many times and in various ways, but in these last days he has spoken to us by his Son, whom he appointed heir of all things" (Heb. 1:1). The latter revelation is superior to the former in every way and supersedes it. For instance, if the former provided for ritual cleansing, how much more the latter would cleanse "our consciences from acts that lead to death, so that we may serve the living God!" (9:14).

William Johnsson comments on the significance of blood sacrifice to traditional peoples: Three theories concerning the motivation for bloody sacrifices converge to a single point with

the desire for life. The 'communion' theory seeks to restore or maintain life

> by participation in divine life; the 'gift' theory seeks the impartation of divine life as reciprocation of the life of the giver imparted in his gift; the 'cosmic rhythm' theory endeavors to renew the vital forces of nature by re-enactment[46]

Here, at the point of convergence, we confront chaos as a threat to existence. We must find a means to overcome it, or it will overcome us.

Sacrifice provides the means. From ritual perspective, it allows us to celebrate success--qualified as it may be. From a functional perspective, it permits us to act in confidence that God honors our efforts. From a religious perspective, we enter into a resilient relationship with the Almighty.

Scripture satisfies this concern for life with the resurrection of Jesus as the earnest of our own. Paul consequently affirms: "But Christ has indeed been risen from the dead, the firstfruits of those who have fallen asleep" (1 Cor. 15:20). His crucifixion and resurrection would subsequently come to be viewed as virtually one saving event, as death-unto-life.

We may look at this once for all event more closely in chaos perspective. We read that there was darkness over all the land from the sixth until the ninth hour (Matt. 27:45). Perhaps due to an eclipse or dust storm, but certainly to remind us of God's displeasure. Chaos had cast its long shadow over Calvary.

Jesus encountered death at the cross. His disciples had for the most part fled the scene; some who passed by mocked Him; He felt the pain of extended torment; He experienced alienation for others; He also sensed life slipping away; at long last the ordeal was over.

Three days passed. He rose from the dead, leaving behind an empty tomb. This was the final sign introduced by John to attest for Jesus' saving ministry. We can be assured by the empty tomb and resurrection appearances, to which may be added the confirmation of faith.

The once for all event was deemed vicarious. He offered Himself *unblemished to God* on behalf of others. The righteous for the unrighteous, that righteousness might be imputed to those who believe.

When sensing the stealthy approach of death, Jesus cried out: "My God, my God, why have you forsaken me?" (Mt. 27:46). Jesus' awareness that His mission would end in death and involve the bearing of the sins of others would "from God was not possible for a perfect man whose mind was wholly committed to the fulfillment of God's will. In this case it must have been an acute consciousness of the extent and meaning of his vicarious suffering that caused intense distress of dereliction."[47]

The once for all event was also thought efficacious. It succeeded where all else had failed. "The former regulation is set aside because it was weak and useless, and a better hope is introduced, by which we draw near to God" (Heb. 7:18)

The lyrics of Augustus Toplady resonate with our thinking: "Not the labors of my hands can fulfill thy law's demands; could my zeal no respite know, could my tears forever flow, all for sin could not atone; thou must save and thou alone." After this, his refrain: "Rock of Ages, cleft for me, let me hide myself in thee" (*Rock of Ages*). When the chaotic storms of life reach gale force, there is a secure shelter beckoning.

Such is the experience of those who face chaos with confidence. Come what will, God appears sovereign. Come what will, God's love remains constant.

LIFE TOGETHER

From early times Noah's ark was seen as a type of the church. Both alike served as a sanctuary for God's people. Both alike ride above the crest of the waves to preserve those within from the chaotic conditions that prevail without.

We pick up with Hendrikus Berkhof to explore this topic in some detail. He suggests six ecclesiastical characteristics: as communion with Christ, recipients of grace, accepted but altered, in communion with one another, not precluding other communities, and experiencing heightened tension.[48]

(1) *The church experiences communion with Christ.* We come to life together *through* Christ. We continue to experience life together *in* Him.

Christ is the door. There are no alternatives.

Christ is the bread of life. There is no other means of sustenance.

Christ is the head. There is none to rival His authority.

Christ is the body. There is no separate identity.

We commune with Christ along with others. It is a corporate exercise. We pray to *our* Father, for *our* daily needs, *our* forgiveness, and *our* deliverance. When on suffers, all suffer; when one rejoices, all rejoice. We are bonded together with Him for time and eternity.

(2) *The church is recipient of God's saving grace.* "For it is by grace you have been saved, through faith--and this not of yourselves, it is the gift of God--not of works so that no one can boast" (Eph. 2:8-9). What the apostle means to say is that the entire project is the result of divine initiative and enablement.

Conversely, the church does not advocate cheap grace. It does not sell fire insurance. The issue, after all the partisan debate has subsided, does not concern grace *or* works, but grace that works.

(3) *The church is a community of the accepted but altered.* Persons have long pondered the dynamic by which Christ altered the lives of those around Him. The Pharisees were certainly not adverse to accepting *sinners*, providing they demonstrated their sincerity. However, Jesus appears to accept persons by way of making them over. It is as if He recognized them for what they might and would become, and thereby

helped them achieve His purpose.

C.S. Lewis was likely thinking along the above line when he observed that God does not accept us because we are so lovable, but because He is so loving. It is because He loves us that He attempts to make us lovable. As sometimes characterized, His is *hard love*.

(4) *The church provides communion among its members.* If one in Christ, then one with each other. Paul comments: "So in Christ we who are many form one body, and each member belongs to all the others" (Rom. 12:5). There are many gifts, but each should be exercised with regard to the fellowship. Even though the tasks may seem demanding, they should be undertaken in good spirit.

"But everything should be done in a fitting and orderly way" (1 Cor. 14:40). As would characterize those who worship in spirit and in truth, not in the chaotic way of competition, but so as to edify one another.

(5) *The church does not preclude participation in other communities.* It uniquely serves God's redemptive strategy; it alone is charged with passing on a sacred heritage; it alone assumes the responsibility to call for repentance and faith; it alone provides the context in which faith can be shared and nurtured. Perhaps it is for these reasons that it can best appreciate community fostered wherever found.

In any case, the church encourages a vibrant participation in the home, in education, at work, in political activity, and in a wide variety of voluntary associations. It certainly does not want to compound the problems of society by distancing itself, or putting a burden on society as a whole.

(6) Finally, *the church creates a heightened tension.* The above scenario cultivates tension by being *in* but not *of* the world. It senses as no other the contradiction between God's will and man's ways. It must bear with misunderstanding, misgivings, and malice.

It draws solace in participating with Christ in His sufferings. The servant cannot hope to expect something other than his Master. It is sufficient that he be treated as His Master.

Even within the fellowship, there are tensions resulting from the need to strive for holiness while maintaining unity, differences of opinion zealously promoted, and from immaturity disguised as piety. Perhaps these are more difficult to bear, since we expect more from those of the household of faith. Even so, we need to keep in mind that God is not through working with us; we are a vessel in the making.

In the above fashion, the ark-typical church negotiates the rising flood waters. Chaos lashes at its bulkhead but it rides the threatening waves until it reaches a safe harbor.

As for the rest, Peter has a sobering thought. "For it is time for judgment to begin with the family of God," he writes, "and if it begins with us, what will the outcome be for those who do not obey the gospel of God?" (1 Pet. 4:17). It appears from chaos imagery, as discussed to this point, grim indeed.

LIGHT AND DARKNESS

Once, when the world was still formless and empty, darkness covered it like a mantle. Then God mandated that there be light, and there was light. The analogue shifts:

> Light has come into the world, but men loved darkness instead of light because their deeds were evil. Everyone who does evil hates the light, and will not come into the light for fear that his deeds will be exposed. But whoever lives by the truth comes into the light, so that it may be seen plainly that what he has done has been done through God (John 3:19-21).

Time passed, and we find Jesus and His disciples gathered in the upper room. Whereupon Jesus was troubled, and observed: "I tell you the truth, one of you is going to betray me" (John 13:21). His disciples were puzzled. Jesus continued: "It is the one to whom I will give this piece of bread I have dipped in the dish." Having dipped, He gave it to Judas Iscariot.

"What you are about to do, do quickly," Jesus instructed Judas. John records that the latter went out, "and it was night." No doubt it was actually night, but for John this symbolized the darkness that grips men's souls.

Jesus had come to dispel that darkness, as His own peculiar task and as shared with others. He subsequently met with His disciples in Galilee, where He announced: "All authority in heaven and earth is given to me. Therefore go and make disciples of all nations" (Matt. 28:18-19). They were to be heralds of light, penetrating the darkness in the course of their ministry.

They were to begin with Jerusalem, work their way through Judea and Samaria, and extend their witness to the ends of the earth. "The Christian teacher who addressed himself to devout Jews had the way to some extent prepared for him. He found in his hearers a strict monotheistic faith,

commonly some kind of Messianic expectation and always a belief
in God's law and in the moral requirements of religion."[49] They were
heirs of the prophets.

Repent and believe, Peter urged his hearers. Turn from chaotic
darkness to the way that grows still brighter with each step along the way.
Do not repeat the folly of Noah's contemporaries, who perished in the
waters; nor of the folk who feared to enter the promised land and were
buried in the wilderness.

The Gentiles provided a different kind of challenge to the disciples.
Herewith, they faced

> a world which did not know Judaism or which hated and despised it, a world
> which was unacquainted with the prophets and familiar with cults not
> pretending to exclusiveness, with mystics not requiring a moral standard of
> their leaders, with an unchangeable and immoral order of destiny determined,
> or at least indicated, by the stars, and magic of various kinds.[50]

It was a world that had shed much of the light which it had once enjoyed.

John skillfully weaves three motifs together in his gospel narrative: the
signs, rejection, and acceptance. First, there were the signs. "Jesus did
many other miraculous signs in the presence of his disciples, which are
not recorded in this book. But these are written that you may believe that
Jesus is the Christ, the Son of God, and that believing you may have life
in his name" (20:30-31).

Second, there was rejection. Why was Jesus rejected? John cites two
considerations, and a third by implication. He alludes to a prophecy by
Isaiah concerning the blindness which has befallen Israel (12:38-40), as
if to remind his readers that this ought not to have come as any surprise.
It had happened time and again throughout the history of his people, that
they have chosen darkness rather than light. A disposition once cultivated
performs on cue.

"Yet at the same time many even among the leaders believed in him, but
because of the Pharisees they would not confess their faith for fear they
would be put out of the synagogue, for they loved praise from men more
than praise from God" (12:42-43). As is often the case, persons fail to
speak out for fear that they will be ostracized and subjected to ridicule.

It was also evident that opposition to Jesus had been building for some
time. He refused to embrace the Zealot political portrait of the Messiah;
He did not share in the separatistic spirit of the Essenes; He took issue
with the Pharisee's expounding of Torah; He challenged the Saduccees'

management of the cult. His followers were largely from among the common folk rather than the power brokers of the Hebrew society.

John wrote in retrospect: "He came to that which was his own, but his own did not receive him" (1:1). While Jesus and His early disciples were without exception Jews, Jewish rejection had become sufficiently normative so that John would use *the Jews* as synonymous with unbelief. Jesus, born of a Jewish mother in the Jewish homeland, was largely rejected by His kinsfolk.

Third, there was acceptance. Curiously, His message was better received by *sinners*. That is, by those who by reason of vocation and/or disposition were not meticulous in religious matters. They had felt ostracized by the religious establishment. They responded heartily to Jesus' uninhibited approach.

The *multitude* that thronged around Jesus were a mixed lot. Some were earnest seekers, and others caught up in the excitement of the moment. Jesus *disciples* were drawn from the multitude, and stood apart. John concludes that any may come to Jesus regardless of past or present circumstances. Whosoever will may come; whoever comes will be gladly received; whoever is received will be blessed. They shall walk in the light, as children of the light, in the midst of a dark and threatening (chaotic) world.

Moreover, they would link together. Light with light, to show the way more perfectly. Light with light, so as to dispel the darkness.

MARANATHA

The term *Maranatha* is perhaps best understood as an imperative: "Our Lord, come!" (cf. 1 Cor. 16:22). The devout pilgrim must contend with the world, the flesh, and the Devil. The *world* acts as an incumbrance. "Therefore, since we are surrounded by such a great cloud of witnesses," Hebrews concludes, "let us throw off everything that hinders and the sin that so easily entangles, and let us run with perseverance the race marked out for us" (12:1).

The *flesh* reminds us of the enemy within. Jewish writers refer to this as the evil *yetzer* (inclination). The rabbis reported that if we tolerate the evil yetzer for even a moment, it will eventually gain full control over our lives. We repulse the evil yetzer by meditating and acting on God's teaching.

As for the *Devil*, we are reminded of the cosmic dimension of our struggle. "For our struggle is not (only) against flesh and blood," Paul reminds his Ephesian audience, "but against the ruler, against the authorities, against the powers of this dark (chaotic) world and against the spiritual forces of evil in the heavenly realms" (6:12). Such being the case, he urged them to put on the full armor of God, so that when the evil day comes, they might be able to stand their ground.

Not surprisingly, the pilgrim concludes that this world is not his home. He/she looks toward the future with the return of Christ. "He who testifies to these things says, 'Yes, I am coming soon.' Amen. Come Lord Jesus" (Rev. 22).

The dawn will soon break. Even now we can see the streaks of light dispelling the darkness. "For the Lord himself will come down from heaven, with a loud command, with the voice of the archangel and with the triumphant call of God" (I Thess. 4:16). As would a military commander, whose order is echoed by subordinates and attended by fanfare. The *Same One* as before will come but in marked contrast to His birth as a child in a stable.

Paul wished to inform his readers as to what they might expect: "We do not want you to be ignorant" (v. 13). It was their legacy as sons of God to know of their inheritance.

He also wanted to comfort those who had lost loved ones. "If Jesus wept at the grave side of his beloved friend Lazarus, his disciples are surely at liberty to do the same. What Paul prohibits is not grief but hopeless grief, not all mourning but mourning *like the rest of men, who have no hope*, that is, like the pagans of his day."[51] "After that, we who are still alive and are left will be caught up together with them in the clouds to meet the Lord in the air. And so we will be with the Lord forever" (v. 17).

The apostle hoped his readers consequently would set their priorities in order. As for him, what once he had considered of worth seemed no more than rubbish in order that he might know Christ, the fellowship of His suffering, the power of His resurrection, righteousness through faith, and deliverance from death. Elsewhere, Paul admonished: "Set your hearts on things above," where Christ is seated at the right hand of God (Col. 3:1), and from which He will return in glory.

Once the priorities are in order, set high standards for achievement. "Do you not know that in a race all the runners run, but only one gets the prize? Run in such a way as to get the prize" (1 Cor. 9:24).

Having entered the race, press on to its conclusion. Get a good start, run hard, and finish strong. Paul confidently concludes: "I have finished the race, I have kept the faith. Now there is in store for me the crown of righteousness, which the Lord, the righteous Judge, will award to me on that day--and not only to me, but also to all who have longed for his appearing" (2 Tim. 4:7-8). He advocated no less for others than he anticipated for himself.

Christ's return eventuates in a new heaven and earth, and new Jerusalem descending out of heaven (cf. Rev. 21:1-2).

> This is a reality which we cannot visualize; but direct, unmarred fellowship between God and his peoples is the goal of all redemption. ...All the promises of God's covenant with men, made first through Abraham, renewed through Moses, and embodied in Christ, are at last brought to full realization.[52]

The celestial Potter will complete the good work once begun. It matters not how many times He must recast His clay. The chaos/order plays out until the final curtain falls..

Then, there will be no more sea, night (darkness), death, or pain. Such allusions to chaos cease. In their place and succinctly put, we have *shalom* (sometimes characterized as peace with justice). God's rule will be universal, uncontested, and everlasting.

"Now we see but a poor reflection as in a mirror; then we shall see face to face" (1 Cor. 13:12). The mirror to which the apostle refers was of polished metal and given to distortion. While in this life, our view of eternal things is at best blurred. The time shall come when what was indistinct will become crystal clear, as when we see someone face to face. Till then, the pilgrimage of faith continues unabated.

EPILOGUE

We begin to tie things together. Or, as otherwise put, to recover the forest from the trees (the general from the particular).

Chaos appears in Scripture at the outset, and as a reoccurring phenomena. It pervades life. We cannot hope to escape chaos, but must learn to deal creatively and constructively with it.

When first introduced to chaos, it resembles the potter casting his clay. After this, he will fashion a vessel. Order follows chaos.

Unless, of course, something goes wrong. Then, the potter will recast his clay, and begin over. Chaos follows order.

We ought not to invite chaos. It will come soon enough. When it does, we ought to use the opportunity to learn God's ways more perfectly. It brings to mind a visit I payed to a hospital patient. "I suppose you are praying to get out of here in short order," I remarked, being at a loss as to what to say. He thought for a moment before responding: "No, I have been praying that I would not leave until I had learned what God would have me know from the experience." I was thoroughly impressed by his piety and wisdom.

Even so, we ought not to unnecessarily extend the chaos experience. As suggested earlier, we press on through the wilderness to the promised land. Anything less would be to draw back from God's leading.

Scripture characterizes this *emerging order* in two ways. First, it is *providential*. God works for our good. He invites us to cooperate with Him.

Second, it is *redemptive*. God would deliver us from our bondage to sin. He would set our feet on high ground. With such in mind, the psalmist petitions: "Rescue me from the mire, do not let me sink; deliver me from those who hate me, from the deep waters" (69:14).

There are usually harbingers of impending chaos. Life as we have experienced it begins to come apart. We build our defenses higher in hopes of buying time. In the end, it is to no avail.

Once order begins to emerge, it needs to be cultivated. As the saying goes, "Rome was not built in a day." Nothing worthwhile comes easily, and especially when it involves charting a new course.

Chaos, in Biblical perspective, involves a mix of *referents*. These occur individually or in some combination. They are sometimes obvious, and on other occasions exceedingly subtle.

The *sea* is a prime referent. It recalls the primordial condition when the Spirit of God was hovering over the waters (Gen. 1:2). This was reenforced by the deluge in Noah's time, when a generation perished because of its wickedness. Visually, the storms off the sea, and erosion of land were a reminder of chaos reality.

The *wilderness* is another referent. It too ties back into the creation account. We read that the earth was formless and empty, and inhospitable to life. Such comes to mind when we leave Jerusalem for Jericho, making our way through the Judean Wilderness. One wastes no time in negotiating the distance to the oasis City of the Palms, where water from Elijah's Spring awaits the thirsty traveler.

Silence is yet another. It recalls at time before God spoke to bring order out of chaos. When God no longer spoke through prophets, it was as if chaos had returned. When God again spoke, it was as if a new order was begun.

Darkness is a reoccurring referent. It recalls a time before God said: "Let there be light, and there was light" (Gen. 1:3). John in particular singles out the darkness/light motif to symbolize the struggle between the evil of this world and the good breaking in with Jesus and the gospel.

Death serves as a final vivid referent. God warned Adam that should he eat of the tree of knowledge of good and evil he would certainly die. He ate and perished as predicted.

Adam lived toward death, as do we. We sense our mortality on every hand: with sickness, disregard, importunity, and advancing age. Life seems brief. Here today, it is gone tomorrow.

While prominent, the above do not exhaust the means by which Scripture alludes to chaos. Some means are more or less explicit, and others characteristically subtle. The more one reads from a chaos perspective, the more evident it becomes that chaos imagery is pervasive.

As for now, we live by the grace of God. Regardless of the circumstances, God's grace abounds. Paul concludes: "I have learned the secret of being content in any and every situation, whether well fed or hungry, whether living in plenty or in want. I can do everything through him who gives the strength" (Phil. 4:12-13).

The apostle spoke from experience. He had learned to cope with chaos. In so doing, he learned to cope with life.

What is the future of chaos theory, and its relevance for religious studies? It is hard to say. Barry Parker's speculation is as good as any, and better than most. He writes: "Despite the tremendous advances that have been made, chaos theory still has defects. One of its most serious is that it does not specify the set of circumstances needed for a given sequence of events to end in chaos."[53] It is as a tool in need of continued refinement.

Then, too, what may be beyond chaos? Parker supposes that it could be complexity. He reasons as follows: "Chaos shows us that simple systems sometimes produce very disorganized behavior. Complexity, on the other hand, shows us that complicated behavior, or complicated rules, sometimes gives organized behavior."[54]

Another area that has been getting increasing consideration is the *edge of chaos,* i.e., the border area between chaos and order. Here fractals come into play, inviting our further investigation.

Parker succinctly sums up: "The phenomenon of chaos has been known for hundreds of years, but the science of chaos is till in its infancy. Scientists have only studied it seriously for the last 30 years. We are still uncertain what the future holds, but optimism is high."[55]

From a theological perspective, we have known of chaos for thousands of years, but have hardly begun to consider it in the light of contemporary chaos theory. It seems that we should welcome a lively discussion, not for fear that someone is invading our privileged domain, but with the conviction that all truth is God's truth.

Part II

Chaos From A Systematic Theology Perspective: Select Instances

Systematic theology attempts to structure religious truth into an organized whole. This can be done in many and varied ways. Some begin with man in his existential condition. Freidrich Schliermacher and Paul Tillich are prime examples.

Others, such as Karl Barth, start with reference to God. These are convinced that we can understand the creature (man) only in connection with its Creator (God). It brings to mind the Biblical assertion that man was created in God's image and for His pleasure.

It is customary for western theologians to preface their discussion of religious content with a consideration of religious authority. This serves a variety of purposes. For one, the Roman Catholic/Protestant polemic over the relationship between Scripture and tradition; for another, in response to the Enlightenment revolt against traditional values; for still another, to counter the *religious enthusiasts* (said to elevate experience over established beliefs).

Cultural bias plagues the task of the systematic theologian. He/she tends to minimize if not exclude what seems irrelevant. Conversely, he/she is inclined to introduce what serves a cultural agenda, even if it has little or no bearing on the source material. All this comes back to haunt us when we attempt to convey our message in a cross-cultural setting.

We have selected two instances to illustrate the pertinence of chaos theory for systematic theology. The first relates to a theological understanding of man, and the other concerning the Holy Spirit. These complement one another in that man was said to be created in God's image. They also invite a more comprehensive treatment in another context and at a future point in time.

CHAOS ANTHROPOLOGY

> The science of chaos is like a river that has been fed from many streams. Its sources come from every discipline--mathematics, physics, chemistry, engineering, medicine and biology, astronomy and meteorology, from those who study fluids and those who study electrical circuits, from strict and rigorous powers of theorems, and from swashbuckling computer experiments.[56]

Not to exclude from the mix, it also comes from theology, sometimes described as *the Queen of the Sciences*.

Where previously we looked at chaos in the context of Biblical theology, here we turn to consider an aspect of systematic theology. In so doing, we turn from a historical to philosophic orientation. There is order to both, but (as noted earlier) the former more resembles that found in nature, and the latter in the nursery.

Man as Creatively Designed

"So God created man in his own image, in the image of God he created him, male and female he created them" (Gen. 1:27). Man serves as a capstone to God's design of an ecological habitat, where once there had been only formless void.

(1) *Chaos appears initially as a preliminary step in creation.* It resembles a lump of clay which the potter sets before him in anticipation of making a vessel for functional use and artistic beauty. As observed above, this is not uncommon in traditions concerning the High God.

We have in systematics been inclined to emphasize the redemptive formula for well-being (*shalom*) to the relative exclusion of celebration and stewardship. Walter Brueggemann would have us restore a balance. He reminds us that the celebration/ stewardship theme can be found not only in the creation account, but wisdom and royal texts as well. He comments as follows: "People who have access to the good life do not await gifts. They only celebrate the gifts already given, and seek to preserve them."[57]

Brueggemann extends his discussion to a theology for *haves* and *have nots*: the former in connection with creation responsibilities and the latter as the oppressed calling out to God for deliverance. These coexist in life, rather than one to the exclusion of the other. They remind us of God love for all, and warns us against disregarding any.

(2) *As such, chaos should be recognized as intrinsic to the creative process.* Initially, the artist has only a blank canvas, inexpressive clay, or a block of wood with which to work. This is before a design begins to emerge, as if to satisfy some creative urge.

As a plausible scenario, our individual and collective security seems constantly threatened.

> At a deep level of the mind we fear chaos and strive to control it by maintaining or establishing order. This abhorrence of disorder is transposed, at a philosophical level, into systems of the ought which attempt to comprehend the external world--comprehend in the sense of intellectually understand, as well as in the sense of comprise and embrace.[58]

This abhorrence of disorder also is expressed by the artist through works that symbolize order.

We seek in these and other ways to bring order out of chaos, which implies a willingness to accept chaos as a transient experience. It may prove threatening, as any author knows full well from staring at a blank monitor with his reputation if not livelihood at stake. It also can be invigorating, as one anticipates something novel to come from his/her efforts. Emotions aside, the tolerance of chaos is characteristic of the creative process.

(3) *To resist chaos in this pristine connection reveals a lack of trust in God's faithfulness.* Man's finite character is compounded by his fallen condition. God's ways contrast to his as the heaven is exalted above the earth (Isa. 55:9). Unable to proceed by sight, he must walk by faith.

God leads him by way of the wilderness in the promised land. Even so, the people complained: "We remember the fish we ate in Egypt at no cost--also the cucumbers, melons, leeks, onions and garlic. But now we have lost our appetite; we never see anything but this manna!" (Num. 11:5-6).

They provoked God to anger, serving as a warning to subsequent generations. "Today, if you hear his voice, do not harden your hearts as you did in the rebellion," when your fathers were denied the promised rest (Heb. 3:7-11). "We cannot know what intends to accomplish in spite of human failures; nor can we know how far God intends, within and through history, to change human nature. Prophetic hope must be absolutely open because it is based on the faith that God is absolutely powerful and good."[59] We are consequently called upon to embrace chaos within God's providential care.

(4) *We hope not to prolong chaos unnecessarily.* The chosen people were not meant to settle in the wilderness, but pass through it. The religious recluse might also be advised to reconsider what may amount to an extension of the wilderness sojourn. God would have us get on with serving others, rather than squandering piety on ourselves. "Like every prophet after Moses, he (Jesus) was unimpressed with the claims of legitimacy made by the institutions of order. ...This does not mean that he was an anarchist. He was not for chaos, but believed unjust political and economic arrangements were falsely legitimated emodiments of chaos."[60] He viewed them as perpetuating chaos in the guise of order, and thereby inhibiting the breaking in of God's kingdom.

From the foregoing, we derive three alternatives: conform to, eliminate, or transform the existing order. Jesus' opposition chose the first of these, the anarchist the second, and Jesus the third. Or in the words of Jesus: "Neither do men pour new wine into old wineskins. ...No, they pour new wine into new wineskins, and both are preserved" (Matt.9:17).

As such, Jesus called for justice, righteousness, and mercy in place of special privilege and oppression. His accent reminds us of the prophetic appeal: "But let justice roll on like a river, righteousness like a never-failing stream!" (Amos 5:24). Moreover, it recalls the prophetic complaint: "For I desire mercy, not sacrifice, and acknowledgment of God rather than burnt offerings" (Hos. 6:6).

Jesus' adversaries hoped to retain the *status quo,* and the privilege it offered. They would determined to do so even at the expense of others. Even so, their time was running out. The old would give way to the new order, with chaos serving as a transition.

(5) *Yet with due patience, so as to learn all that God would teach us during the interim.* There is much we can learn about ourselves and others, the circumstance that surround us, and the grace of God freely extended on our behalf.

The principle that a human being is sacred yet morally degraded is hard for common sense to grasp. It is apparent to everyone that some people are morally degraded. It is ordinarily assumed, however, that other people are morally upright and that those alone possess dignity. From this point of view, all is simple and logical.[61]

Simple and logical to be sure, but also misleading. We see this erroneous perception in to the Marxist dogma of class struggle, colonial rationalization of cultural superiority, and the good guy bad guy dichotomy perpetuated by Western films. Such hold little tolerance for those who disagree, and are too uncritical of those who do. Chaos proves devastating to our pretense. We are pressed to face up to reality: not uncommonly what we have failed to admit concerning ourselves and what we have been reluctant to grant others.

We also discover what it means to live in God's world, and by His grace. As a friend graphically puts it, this world is *God's sandbox*. We had best learn to play by His rules.

Three times Paul plead with the Almighty to take away his thorn in the flesh, but received instead the assurance: "My grace is sufficient for you, for my power is made perfect in weakness" (2 Cor. 12:9). Whereupon, the apostle concluded: "That is why, for Christ's sake, I delight in weaknesses, in insults, in hardships, in persecutions, in difficulties. For when I am weak, then I am strong." So we learn in patiently enduring chaos as a a providential tool in God's hand.

As if to summarize all the above: "God is our refuge and strength, and ever-present help in trouble. Therefore we will not fear, thought the earth give way and the mountains fall into the heart of the sea (graphic chaos symbolism)" (Psa. 46:1-3). There is a river whose streams bring rejoicing to the city of God, as if eternal order emerging from resilient chaos.

Man In Rebellion

God remonstrated with Adam: "Because you listened to your wife and ate from the tree about which I commanded you, 'You must not eat of it,' cursed is the ground because of you; through painful toil you will eat of it all the days of your life" (Gen. 3:17). With these and other words, Adam was introduced to the grievous nature of his offense and its appalling results.

(6) *We may capriciously disregard order, inviting chaos to return.* Scripture portrays man as conditioned to sin, without any precise explanation of how this comes about (cf. Psa. 51:5; Eph. 2:3).

Persons have expounded various theories to account for what the Biblical text leaves uncertain. Some have reasoned that Adam acted as our corporate head, so that all fell with him; others that sin is biologically transmitted; still others that it is socially conditioned.

While not necessarily ruling out any of the above options, chaos theory provides an alternative way of viewing the matter. It may be expressed with reference to *the sensitive dependence on original conditions*, a phenomenon characteristic of nonlinear (complex) systems.

The problem this creates for predicting weather serves as an apt analogy.

> The weather, even this unsimplified model of it, is not susceptible to long-range prediction because it is too sensitive to almost imperceptible changes in the initial conditions, which changes lead to slightly bigger ones a minute later or a foot away, which slightly bigger ones lead to yet more substantial deviations, the whole process cascading over time into a nonrepetitive unpredictability.[62]

Thus some relatively minor disturbance in the Caribbean could reach hurricane force by the time it reaches the American mainland.

Adam's sin could be similarly viewed. Given the sensitivity of nonlinear systems to original conditions, the results could be catastrophic. The dogma of original sin hence becomes eminently plausible from chaos perspective.

Man also appears in Scripture as a sinner by choice (cf. Rom. 1:21, 2:21-22). This has solicited extended debate over the relation of predestination to free will. J. Doyne Farmer comments from chaos perspective: "On a philosophical level, it struck me as an operational way to define free will, in a way that allowed you to reconcile free will with determinism. The system is deterministic, but you can't say what its going to do next."[63] Clinical psychologist Donald Tweedie seems to reach a similar conclusion in a lecture given some years ago. He reasoned that whereas the life process appears deterministic, choice might be understood as one determining factor among others.

This topic deserves more consideration than we can give it in this context. Suffice to say, chaos theory opens up new possibilities for resolving a persisting conundrum.

(7) *Man thus appears as if a pawn in a conflict of cosmic proportions*. The enigmatic serpent assumes the role of tempter. Whereas patristic sources were inclined to identify it *as* Satan, there seems no compelling warrant for doing so. While said to be related to Canaanite fertility cults,

this connection also seems after the fact.

The *Gilgamesh Epic* no doubt provides us with the most striking literary parallel. It relates how Gilgamesh found a plant through which he could avoid death. It came to pass that while he was swimming, a snake made off with the plant and thereby robbing him of immortality. "Here in Geneses we have a quite different story, but once again a snake, man, plants, and the promise of life are involved, though here man loses immortality through blatant disobedience, whereas in the epic that loss seems to be just a matter of bad luck."[64]

Not to be overlooked, the serpent in antiquity also symbolized chaos. Chaos, in turn, alerts us to a nonlinear system. Such as when an astronomer observes a planet taking a curious course, he assumes an unseen satellite must be implicated. With more careful investigation, he finds his surmise accurate.

Here the culprit is revealed to be an adversarial spirit active in the world. Paul summarily concludes: "For our struggle is not against flesh and blood, but against the rulers, against the authorities, against the powers of this dark world and against the spiritual forces of evil in the heavenly realms" (Eph. 6:12).

As chaos alerts us to a nonlinear system, the latter in turn alerts us to the former. We may expect chaos to return from time to time in the real world as depicted by Scripture. We must learn how to creatively work with chaos or fail in our endeavor.

(8) *We further compound the problem through chronic mistrust, disobedience, and pretentious social engineering.* The core of sin is unbelief, whether concerning Adam and Eve or their posterity. Failing to put our trust in God, we chose rather to shift for ourselves.

The opposite of sin, conceived as unbelief, is not virtue as such but faith. Paul expressed the faith ideal when he observed that "in all things God works for the good of those who love him, who have been called according to his purpose" (Rom. 8:28).

Sin may take the form of commission or omission. It qualifies in either case as disobedience. You shall not murder, commit adultery, steal, or bear false testimony; for in so doing we sin. You shall love God without qualification, and your neighbor as yourself; for in failing to do so we sin.

"The Christian life is characterized by obedience to the law, which basically means keeping the commandments. But is also marked by striving to live up to the law of love, which is the highest commandment. It is not faith alone but faith perfected by love that is the hallmark of life in the Spirit."[65]

It is not unbelief alone, but unbelief expressed in disobedience that characterizes depravity.

The ancients encouraged one another: "Come, let us build ourselves a city, with a tower that reaches to the heavens, so that we may make a name for ourselves" (Gen. 11:3-4). Primal history thus reaches its fruitless climax with man endeavoring to glorify his own achievement through corporate endeavor.

This can be seen in the way social engineering fosters privilege and frustrates justice. Embracing chaos in institutional form, it assures its own destruction. Like a tower of cards, it awaits God's breath to topple it into a heap.

(9) *We thus inhibit our potential for good, our prior decisions coming to dominate life.* One ought not to blame society, even though society expresses and reinforces the primal decision to sin. We have no one or nothing to blame but ourselves. We have met the enemy, and he is *us*.

In chaos jargon, nonlinear systems "often behave quite normally and smoothly for a wide range of initial conditions and then suddenly become chaotic when a parameter of the system attains a critical value."[66] Sin wears away original resolve until we are incapable of resisting and life come unglued.

Two contrasting ways stretch out before us: the way of life and death. The way of life resembles a narrow path leading into ever broader opportunities; the latter a broad road narrowing to the point that we have no leeway. What may at first may seem constricting proves to be enriching. Conversely, what previously appears liberating results in bondage. Such is life's paradox from the perspective of Scripture.

Sometimes there is little high ground from which to operate. At such times, we ought not to expect too much too soon. Capture some point of advantage even though it hardly seems worth the effort. This will open up more promising possibilities, more readily available.

(10) *We also invite God's wrath, expressed by a return to chaos conditions.* "I looked at the earth, and it was formless and empty, and at the heavens, and their light was gone. ...I looked, and the fruitful land was a desert, all its towns lay in ruins before the Lord, before his fierce anger" (Jer. 4:23, 26).

The people had refined their skill with doing evil, but gave no indication of insight into doing good (v. 22). Thus they invited God's wrath, and when He seemed disinclined, they demanded it.

When at last God's wrath was manifest, it seemed as if a scorching wind from off the dessert. Life withered on the vine. Persons looked in one direction or another for an escape.

Some fled into the thickets and others climbed among the rocks. All the towns were deserted (v. 27). Social life had collapsed.

The whole land lay in ruin (v. 27). There was desolation on every hand. Nature was scared beyond recognition.

"Sin, then, accomplishes the opposite of what it intends. It begins in self-exaltation. It ends in indignity and death."[67] It repudiates the way of God, and invokes instead His wrath.

Even so, God promises not to utterly destroy the land (v. 27). Herewith, we "come to realize that the wrath of God, though real, is simply a form of God's love that will not desist until the sinner is turned to the way of life and salvation."[68] Either this or man resists to the bitter end. In the latter, C.S. Lewis reminds that God knows when an extension of time will no longer serve any constructive purpose.

R.K. Harrison's commentary serves as a cogent summary: "The dirt and clutter in Jerusalem's streets are but one symptom of her spiritual malaise. Jeremiah anticipates Diogenese of Greece in his quest for an honest man. But none can be found, whether in private houses or in public in the city squares."[69]

Man As Beloved

"Though we are slaves," Ezra encouraged his associates, "our God has not forsaken us" (9:9). Whoever the people and whatever their circumstances, God has not forsaken them. However viewed by others, God has not forsaken them.

(11) *God's love would henceforth be expressed in and through a fallen world.* It is love *in situ* (in location), not expressed in ideal but realistic terms. It is also *ambiguous* in that sin distorts both the manner of expression and our perception of it.

Take the example of a parent who must reprimand a child. A reprimand in and of itself would not seem an expression of love. It is nonetheless the case given the circumstances.

As for the child, it may be difficult to convince him/her of the parent's genuine affection. We are loath to embrace responsibility or accept our guilt. We have become adept in rationalization, further distorting our perception.

While the scriptures provide many instances of what may be designated as *situated love,* one illustration may suffice. We recall that the Hebrew monarchy was not established as a divine mandate but in response to a rebellious peoples' desire to emulate the behavior of the pagan nations around them (cf. 1 Sam. 8).

The monarchy appears inconsistent with the early Israelite ideal of a free society of equals individually and collectively responsible for their covenant obligations. "God maintained his direct rule by raising up charismatic leaders as he chose, rather than sanctioning a dynasty. Such leaders, for all their failings, were much less liable than hereditary monarchs to forget either their solidarity with the people or their responsibility to God."[70] Even so, we recall the period of the judges as being exceedingly chaotic. Under what might seem the best of options, things continued to unravel.

Transition to a monarchy was perhaps inevitable. In any case, it was anticipated (Deut. 17:14-20).

The monarchy fostered an unresponsive bureaucracy, and the growth of social and economic inequality. Which, in turn, solicited the ire of the prophets. They took as their task to fine-tune the monarchy to its covenant ideal.

The Old Testament does not prescribe

> a particular political system for later societies. What if does provide us is a criterion for assessing all political systems and their practice: that government must be exercised on behalf of all the people, in the interests of all, and especially in the interests of those who would otherwise suffer most, the weakest and most disadvantage.[71]

In one manner and/or another, would God express His perfect love through an imperfect society.

(12) *Our experience with chaos reveals remarkable order of comprehensive and providential character.* This much appears certain: "Here was order, with randomness emerging, and then one step further away was randomness with its underlying order."[72] Reality proves to be more complex than earlier imagined. "As physicists have already found through quantum mechanics, the full structure of the world is richer than our language can express and our brains comprehend. Many deep problems remain open for exploration, but at least we have made a start (with chaos reasoning)."[73]

Chaos theory leaves considerable room for conjecture. Scripture nonetheless encourages us to believe in divine provident justice. God "works out everything in conformity with the purpose of his will" (Eph.

1:11). "He makes nations great, and destroys them; he enlarges nations, and disperses them" (Job 12:23).

Pascal's famous wager seems more convincing in chaos perspective than ever before. If God exists, we have all to gain in this life and that to come. If not, we have experienced the best that life has to offer. If however we fail to wager, we lose everything.

(13) *Faith in divine providence allow us to pick up at any given point in response to divine initiative.* God discovered Abram among an idolatrous people, Moses herding his father-in-law's sheep, and Saul on his way to persecute Christians in Damascus. The rest of their life started from that point on.

It involved a new beginning. The past was left behind. The present looked to the future and God's faithfulness.

It required taking on new responsibilities. These would be revealed with the passing of time. Those who walk by faith take one step at a time.

Chaos theory may provide some insight into the human response to divine initiative.

Novelists too may someday find that fractal analogues in 'psychic space' are helpful in capturing the fractured yet nevertheless coherent structure of human consciousness, whose focus can shift instantaneously from the moment's trivia to timeless verities and then back again, somehow preserving the same persona at the various levels.[74]

It is as if to view life from some vantage point before plunging back into its routine.

As a result, some discover meaning in life, while others seem never to catch on. The former live by the light they have until the way becomes more evident. The latter seem to stumble on, creating problems for themselves and others. Worse still, they assume that this is the way things must be.

(14) *In responding to divine initiative, we become less a part of the problem and more involved in a redemptive resolution.* Since God calls for repentance, it comes it the form of a response. It further appears as the initial response called for (cf. Mk. 1:15; Acts 2:37-38).

Repentance implies a change of mind. The prodigal turns his face homeward in anticipation of improved conditions.

While repentance can be distinguished from faith and conversion, it cannot be separated from them. Those who repent believe, and those who believe repent. Conversion comes in response to repentance/faith.

We are enjoined to bring forth fruit *in keeping with repentance* (Matt.

3:8). The theme reoccurs concerning deceivers who themselves may be deceived (7:15-23; 12:33), and the kingdom bing removed from those who fail to bear fruit and bestowed on those who do (21:33).

Subsequent conduct requires living out the kingdom life in social context. As popularly put, being *in* but not *of* the world.

This involves accepting suffering in a fallen world. While none can escape, the believer embraces suffering confident of God's gracious purposes. He/she thus takes a constructive approach to suffering, and in so doing witness to his/her faith.

"Dear friends," Peter writes, "do not be surprised at the painful trial you are suffering, as thought something strange were happening to you" (1 Pet. 4:12). It should not surprise us since we were prompted to expect it as a result of man's defection. It is not strange in that it is an aspect of life as we experience it.

The believer also suffers for Christ's sake. Paul remonstrated with his accusers: "I have worked much harder, been in prison more frequently, been flogged more severely, and been exposed to death again and again" (2 Cor. 11:23). Such things he gladly embraced in order that by all means, he might save some.

In such ways, we are said to share in the sufferings of Christ (1 Pet. 4:13). Moreover, if not share in His sufferings, then also in His glory. All in all, this is a cause of great rejoicing.

The believer additionally suffers for life together. "Carry each other's burdens" (Gal. 6:2), Paul admonished. Ease the load of others by increasing your own. In this emulate Jesus.

"Rejoice with those who rejoice; mourn with those who mourn" (Rom. 12:14). We assume our place in community for better and worse.

The believer finally suffers in the wilderness. "The wilderness is without visible support, but it is also the place where ample supplies of manna are given every day. ...The trick is to get our minds and hearts off our insecurity and anxiety long enough to trust him."[75] As the saying goes, a pilgrim is one without any means of visible support. He/she unconditionally launches into God's future. Let come what will.

(15) *After all has been said and done, we assert an anthropology for the real world.* We quoted early on from Ian Percival's article "Chaos: A Science for the Real World." Chaos theorists have repeatedly echoes his conviction, drawing on familiar illustrations from the natural and social sciences. Theology joins the other disciples to advocate a realistic appraisal of life.

According to the ever perceptive Pascal:

mythology, a fire belching monster with the head of a lion, the body of a goat, and a serpent's tail), then, is man! What a novelty, what a monster, what a chaos, what a contradiction, what a prodigy! Judge of all things, helpless earthworm, depository of truth, a sink of uncertainty and error. Glory and scum of the universe" (*Pensees*, #131).

What a chimera! Created in the image of God, reflecting something of his noble origin. Creative as well as created. Without focus unless focused in the Almighty.

What a chimera! A rebel without a cause. Turning his back on God. Continuing in his perverse way without thought of the result on himself or others. Leaving behind a trail of destruction.

What a chimera! Fallen but not forsaken. Still the object of God's love. Invited to respond to God's gracious initiatives. By way of God's grace, still redeemable.

There comes to mind in closing Jesus' parable of the prodigal *sons*: one who wasted his inheritance in an alien country and the other who failed to share in his father's unbridled rejoicing with his brother's return. The father reasoned with the latter: "But we had to celebrate and be glad, because the brother of yours was dead and is alive again; he was lost and is found" (Luke 15:32). This turns out to be the best of scenario for man in chaos perspective.

CHAOS PNEUMATOLOGY

Advocates promote chaos as the most current, comprehensive, and satisfactory paradigm yet devised. Said to have originated with Henri Poincare in the late nineteenth century, it has taken flight the last decade.[76]

Ian Percival, as I have reported on other occasions, describes chaos as *a science for the real world.*[77] Percival and associates draw their illustrations from such mundane matters as the dripping of a faucet, kneading of dough, and a leaf negotiating the seemingly erratic behavior of a stream.

In chaos theory, we recognize the interplay of order and chaos. Order surrenders to chaos, and chaos to order. Small deviations earlier on cause successively larger deviations. Complex factors result in unpredictable results.

Chaos is as chaos does. Scripture introduces us to chaos with the creation being without form and void. After that, it turns up in various connections, sometimes clearly obvious and other times in subtle fashion.

We purpose an initial inquiry in pneumatology (the study of the Holy Spirit) from chaos perspective. We will pick our way from *creation*, by way of *retribution*, to *redemption*. These resemble prominent theological peaks along an extended mountain range.

Creation

"Now the earth was formless and empty, darkness was over the surface of the deep, and the Spirit of God was hovering (moving, sweeping) over the waters" (Gen. 1:2). *The Spirit* of God seems a preferable rendering *the mighty wind*, thus in keeping with the use of *Elohim* (God) elsewhere. This assumed, it may be taken as a manifestation of God.

Whether to translate as *wind*, *breath*, or *spirit* may not be of great consequence. The reference appears imprecise, what we sometimes allude to as a *fuzzy-set*. As such, this is where the saga of the Spirit properly begins.

(1) *Spirit and chaos*. We need not assume an early antithesis between Spirit and chaos. Whereas chaos comes to take on a primarily negative connotation, it appears neutral here. The same could be said concerning darkness.

Rachaph (hovering or some alternative) suggests the relation of the Spirit to chaos, and later to describe an eagle hovering over its young. Thus we read that God resembles "an eagle that stirs up its nest and hovers over its young, that spreads its wings to catch them and carries them on its pinions" (Deut. 32:11).

Some preliminary observations seem in order. The Spirit appears as if preparing for a creative venture. Soon chaos would give way to order.

It naturally brings to mind the potter motif (cf. Jer. 18:1-10). The potter first places a formless lump of lay on his wheel, before he begins to fashion into a functional and artistically pleasing vessel. The first step anticipates what is to follow. It serves as a means to an end.

The potter motif is a familiar one in High God traditions. It is refined in some instance, as with the Shilluk, who believe that God chose clay of various colors to account for the differences in pigmentation. In other instances, God selects a piece of wood (as yet without definition), and from that carves His creatures.

I recall watching the Hebron potter affectionately called *the old man* working his trade. He assumed a comfortable position, and cast his clay. He paused for a moment, as if to draw the attention of those standing around. Then, and only then, did his hands being to shape the clay.

Moments later the vessel began to take shape. There were grasps of appreciation from those who observed as the clay responded to the master's touch. When at last he had finished, we concluded that the result was very good (cf. Gen. 1:31). This is the impression one gets from the creation account concerning the Spirit and chaos.

Since chaos is not limited to the primordial situation, we would expect something of the Spirit/chaos original precedent to carry over. Out of chaos, the Spirit fashions life in diversity and so that each aspect would complement every other.

Were God to remove His Spirit, we would suppose life to return to its chaotic character. As when the potter observes that his vessel has a defect, and recasts the clay for subsequent use.

At such times, God does not give up on His labor of love. He simply starts over. He does so in some creative fashion we might never expect.

Jeremiah provides us with a case in point. "I looked at the earth, and it was formless and empty; and a the heavens and their light was gone" (4:23).

> So devastating is the judgment upon Judah that Jeremiah instinctively thinks of the state of primeval chaos, except that what they became 'good' will now be turned to desolation at the divine presence. ...The heedless destruction consequent upon apostasy has brought ruin upon the land, and the skies are darkened in mourning.[78]

Even so, God did not cast His people aside.

> This is what the Lord says: "When seventy years are completed for Babylon, I will come to you and fulfill my gracious promise to bring you back in this place. For I know the plans I have for you," declares the Lord, "plans to proper you and not to harm you, plans to give you hope and a future" (29:10-11).

Order will once again supplant chaos.

(2) *Spirit of God.* It seems best to treat the creation account in context of the Semitic High God traditions. The designation *High God* relates to the supreme deity; whether understood in monotheistic, polytheistic, or henotheistic terms. The meandering of the High God is conveyed in such instances as Abraham's interchange with Melchizedek (Gen. 14:18-20), Daniel's dream interpretation concerning Nebuchadnezzar and the latter's admission (Dan. 4:19-37), and with Paul's commentary on *An Unknown God* (Acts 17:22-31).

Norman Gottwald lists six characteristics of the consensus High God. He exercised comprehensive power; while transcendent, was also active in nature and history; could be expressed through natural and human analogies; was powerful, just, and merciful; might bind Himself to a people or region; and was interpreted by human representative.[79]

These characteristics can be readily illustrated from the Biblical narrative. God exercises comprehensive power: "Heaven is my throne, and the earth is my footstool" (Isa. 66:1); while transcendent, He is active in nature and history: "Then the man and his wife heard the sound of the Lord God as he was walking in the garden in the cool of the day, and they hid from the Lord God among the trees of the garden" (Gen. 3:8); He could be expressed through natural and human analogies: "Since you are my rock and my fortress, for the sake of your name lead and guide me" (Psa. 31:3); He is powerful, just, and merciful: "The Lord, the Lord, the compassionate and gracious God, slow to anger, abounding in love and faithfulness, maintaining love to thousands, and forgiving wickedness, rebellion and sin" (Exod. 34:4-7); He might bind Himself to a people or region: "Leave your country, your people, and your father's household and go to the land I will show you" (Gen. 12:1); He is interpreted by human representatives: "Afterward Moses and Aaron went to Pharaoh and said, 'This is what the Lord, the God of Israel says,' "Let my people go, so that they may hold a festival to me in the desert"'" (Exod. 5:1).

Since we think of the High God as transcendent, His Spirit would appear mysterious in His working. Jesus confirmed this to Nicodemus: "The wind blows wherever it pleases. You hear its sound, but you cannot tell where it comes from or where it is going. So it is with everyone born of the Spirit" (John 3:8).

While mysterious, He acts forcefully. "I know you can do all things," Job allowed; "no plan of yours can be thwarted" (42:1). The Spirit appears as if the executor of God's irresistible will.

We are left with only two options. We can cooperate or serve His purpose involuntarily. As C.S. Lewis put it, either as *sons or tools of God.*

(3) *Spirit and word.* "So is my word that goes out from my mouth: It will not return to me empty, but accomplish what I desire and achieve the purpose for which I sent it" (Isa. 55:11). Jewish liturgy refers to the Almighty as "He who spoke and the world came into existence."

"These verses (Gen. 1:3-5) contain the seven standard formulae that comprise the description of each stage of creation: 1) announcement, 'God said'; 2) command, 'let there be'; 3) fulfillment, 'it was so'; 4) execution, 'light'; 5) approval, 'saw...good'; 6) subsequent word, 'God called'; 7) day number."[80] Only here are the seven elements present in a simple sequence.

We can derive several conclusions. What God would do, He can. What God promises to do, He does. Whatever He does is good. These being true, we ought to reverence Him. The psalmist exhorts: :"Let the earth fear the Lord; let all the people of the world revere him. For he spoke, and it came to be" (33:8-9).

Spirit and word appear as a virtual composite in bringing about God's purposes in creation. The former perhaps resembles the creative imagination of the potter, and the latter his expressive hands. They function as one.

The bond carries over with the prophetic office. "For prophecy never had its origin in the will of man, but men spoke form God as they were carried along by the Holy Spirit" (2 Pet. 1:21). They were carried along, as if a ship by wind and current.

While the above text provides the most precise reference to inspiration, it makes no explicit reference to how it is accomplished. The working of the Spirit remains mysterious in this regard as in others.

> Moses was the fountainhead of the prophets, that distinguished assemble of persons who spoke out for God, He, lie those who followed him, challenged the waywardness of men with the unfailing word of liberty and live over against that of bondage and death. They had to decide whether to receive the enablement of the Spirit or grieve Him by their resistance.[81]

They were not allowed to chose between Spirit or word, but embrace both together or reject both together.

With acceptance, the prophets waged a valiant struggle against evil. Even in defeat, their words remained as a testimony against a rebellious people. Even in exile, they remained to comfort the people with the hope of return.

With rejection, the prophets succumbed to the evil around them. They lost their divine leverage. They became mere mortals, and the worse for having squandered their opportunity.

(4) *Spirit and transiency.* We take up the next topic indirectly. The *Gaul* disappeared off the coast of Norway in 1974 with the loss of thirty-six persons. The inquiry did not turn up anything wrong in its design.

> One possible explanation put forward for the loss of the vessel was that it capsized as the result of some transient phenomenon when hit broadside by a short succession of abnormally large waves. 'Transient phenomenon' means that the vessel was moving in an irregular fashion: rocking, swaying, pitching, heaving and rolling.[82]

This was not something that could have been predicted by standard testing. It also serves as a classic illustration of the unpredictable character of chaos reality.

Transiency implies more than motion. It refers to motion that has not as yet settled down into a steady and regular pattern. As such, it offers a way of understanding the creation process.

In any case, the Spirt appears as if peculiarly manifest in chaotic times. C.S. Lewis inadvertently touched on this when he observed that miracles do not appear uniformly in Scripture, but as a rule at critical junctures in redemptive history.

Take the experience of the Hebrew people in Egypt as a prime example. Once Egypt was their sanctuary, but no more. They were oppressed and threatened with genocide. The corporate life was increasingly characterized by chaos.

God was nonetheless at work. Soon He would deliver them so that they might serve Him. Their lives would become regulated by covenant precepts. Were would be called a holy people, living according to their covenant obligation.

Still, the way ahead appeared strange and foreboding. They longed for the security of former and familiar surroundings. A generation perished in the chaotic wilderness, before a new generation possessed the promised land.

Such is the transient character of life. Change is required; not simply change for its own sake but change in keeping with God's initiatives. The Spirit seizes upon such situations to clarify God's ways more perfectly, and strengthen the people of God to do His work.

Retribution

When God saw how corrupt the world had become, He "was grieved that he had made man on the earth, and his heart was filled with pain" (Gen. 6:6). At this, He decided that He would destroy them all, except righteous Noah and his family.

When Noah and family were safely with the ark, God brought a great flood covering the earth. As such, it resembled a return to primordial chaos.

(5) *Spirit and the wrath of God.* With the deluge, we encounter the wrath of God as expressed in His decision to eliminate an evil generation. It springs from an acrid indignation. The root

> is used to express the most intense form of human emotion, a mixture of rage and bitter anguish. Dinah's brothers felt this way after she was raped; so did Jonathan when he heard Gaul's plan to kill David; and David reacted similarly when he heard of Absalom's death (Gen. 34:7; 1 Sam. 20:34; 2 Sam. 19:2).[83]

Yet, only in this instance have we the qualifier *to His heart*, expressing the matchless depth of God's repulsion.

As one would erase a name from the record (Exod. 17:14), God determined to wipe the world clean. Wrath, like other of God's sentiments, is expressed primarily through action." All the nations will ask: 'Why has the Lord done this to this land? Why this fierce, burning anger?'" (Deut. 29:24).

"My Spirit will not contend (abide) with man forever," God averred (Gen. 6:3). Time was running out.

"As it was in the days of Noah, so it will be at the coming of the Son of Man" (Matt. 24:37). They were eating and drinking marrying and giving in marriage, without realizing their impending doom. "No special significance is to be read into these particular participles. They stand merely as indicators of the everyday, ordinary life. The people of Noah's day were oblivious to all else than their own pleasurable living."[84] They experienced pleasure; God experienced pain. They assumed things to continue as they were; God determined it was time for a change. While there was yet time, they lingered. When too late, there was no recourse.

The theme was acted out again with the prophets. Impervious to the Spirit's pleading, people furthered their interests without regard for God's righteous concerns. "God will stretch out over Edom the measuring line of chaos and the plumb line of desolation" (Isa. 34:11). "I looked to the earth, and it was formless and empty; and at the heavens, and their light was gone" (Jer. 4:23).

When at long last Jerusalem was in ruins, the Hebrews reflected on how this had come about. "The crown has fallen from our head," they concluded. "Woe to us, for we have sinned" (Lam. 5:16).

Be encouraged! "For his anger lasts only a moment, but his favor lasts a lifetime; weeping may remain for a night, but rejoicing comes in the morning" (Psa. 30:5). The Spirit not only afflicts the comfortable, but comforts the afflicted.

(6) *Spirit and provision.* "So make yourself an ark of cypress wood," God instructed Noah (Gen. 6:14). A huge box, it was divided to accommodate the creatures that would inhabit it. There were a pair of each for preserving the species, and seven of sacrificial animals.

"That day all the springs of the great deep burst forth, and the floodgates of the heavens were opened" (Gen. 7:11). The waters above and below converged, reversing the creation order (cf. 1:6-10).

As the rains fell, the waters rose. "For forty days the flood kept coming on the earth, and as the waters increased they lifted the ark high above the earth" (v. 17). The water level continued to rise until the mountain peaks were covered. Still it rose another twenty feet.

All the creatures that roamed the earth perished. All those that flew above perished with them. A generation of people were lost. "Only Noah was left, and those with him in the ark" (v. 24).

"Noah did everything just as God commanded him" (v. 22). His thorough obedience was an indication of an unwavering faith. "By faith Noah, when warned about things not yet seen, in holy fear built an ark to save his family. By his faith he condemned the world and became heir of the righteousness that comes by faith" (Heb. 11:7).

The *reality of the unseen* is a prominent theme in this chapter

> as can be seen from the following list: v. 1-things hoped for, but not yet seen, v. 3-creation from what cannot be seen, v. 6-that God exists and rewards, v. 7-events yet unseen, v. 8-an unknown country, v. 10-the city with permanent foundations, v. 13-from a long way off they saw, v. 14-looking for a country, v. 16-the heavenly country, v. 26-kept his eyes on the future reward, v. 27-as though he saw the invisible God. Even beyond those explicit references, it is assumed that the champions of faith referred to in this chapter act as they do because of their full conviction concerning the reality of God and his promises.[85]

"Here was order, with randomness (chaos) emerging, and then one step further away was randomness with its underlying order."[86] So would the flood appear in chaos perspective.

As for the generation that perished, there was no light at the end of the chaos tunnel. There would be no dawn to scatter the chaos darkness.

As for those who survived, the ark symbolized God's provision. Not surprisingly, the church fathers took the ark to typify the church. Both serve as God's refuge in a world bent on self-destruction.

(7) *Spirit and preservation.* God remembered Noah, as He would remember Abraham after the destruction of Sodom (8:1; cf. 19:29). When God remembers, He acts. Once more the *fuzzy-set* wind/Spirit sweeps over the earth. The springs of the deep and the floodgates of the heavens are closed. "The water receded steadily from the earth" (v. 3).

After this, God promised that He would n ever again bring so complete a destruction on the earth. No, "even though every inclination of his (man's) heart is evil from childhood" (v. 21).

> The divine blessing, "Be fruitful and multiply and fill the earth," was again repeated; this time to Noah, his wife, his sons, their wives, and every living thing on the earth, in the air, and on the sea (Gen. 8:17; 9:1, 7). Here God added His special covenant with nature. He would maintain "seedtime, harvest, cold, heat, summer, winter, day, and night" without interruption as

long as the earth remained (8:22). The contents of these promises formed an "everlasting covenant between God and every living creature of all flesh" (9:8, 11, 16). As signified by the rainbow in the sky.[87]

As for the rainbow, it resembled a war bow, lifted overhead as a token of peace.

God's covenant with Noah was exceedingly generous, given its breadth (every living creature), duration (everlasting), and unconditional character. It accents not man's goodness (whose stock had toppled with the flood), but God's unmitigated grace.

The covenant provided a religious and social order. It involved prohibitions against idolatry, blasphemy, murder, improper sexual relations, theft, and the abuse of animals, along with establishing courts of law. These prohibitions, woven into a living fabric, require that we worship God, honor His name, respect life, experience sex within prescribed conditions and treat animals humanely.

Through obedience to the covenant obligations, we shore up our corporate structure. When we ignore them, society begins to fragment. Chaos returns.

The chaos drama will continue until the final curtain drops. We are told that God does not want any to perish, but all to come to repentance (2 Pet. 3:9). C.S. Lewis observes that God knows when time will no longer serve any good purpose. Until then, the Spirit sustains life in a fallen world.

Redemption

The silent years between the Testaments were not uneventful. Conversely, they were chaotic, as evidenced by social upheaval and silence.

At long last, the silence broke with the voice of one calling in the wilderness: "Prepare the way for the Lord, make straight paths for him. ...And all mankind will see God's salvation" (Matt. 3:4, 6). The Messianic Age had dawned.

(8) *Spirit of Christ*. The Spirit was associated with Jesus in His mission from the outset. Thus when Jesus was baptized, He "saw the Spirit of God descending like a dove and lighting on him" (Matt. 3:16). This was accompanied by a voice from heaven announcing: "This is my Son, whom I love; with him I am well pleased."

We need not assume that Jesus had no previous experience of the Spirit; the vision symbolizes his commissioning for his Messianic work, not a anew spiritual status. The *dove* as a symbol of the Spirit was not common in Jewish thought, but is found in some later Jewish writings, based probably on the Spirit's 'hovering' over the waters in Genesis 1:2.[88]

As with the previous instance, Spirit and word combined to signal a new beginning.

"Then Jesus was led by the Spirit into the desert to be tempted by the devil" (Matt. 4:1). We lived for four years in Jerusalem, set in a saddle along a ridge running north and south. To the west, the land falls away into the *shephelah* (foothills), and is nourished by the dew and rain. To the east, it drops abruptly into the wilderness, a region inhospitable to life.

Since God did not create the earth "to be empty, but formed it to be inhabited" (Isa. 45:18), the wilderness corresponds to chaos in its initial and transitory connection. One may have to pass that way to reach his/her destination, but tarries no longer than necessary.

On the other hand, one ought not to rush through the wilderness experience until he/she learns what God would have him/her learn. As the say goes, "man's extremity proves to be God's opportunity."

As with the Hebrew people before Him, Jesus was tested in the wilderness. Unlike them, He succeeded. "Then the devil left him, and angels came and attended him" (v. 11).

"Jesus thereupon returned to Galilee *in the power of the Spirit*. Then, when He had entered into the Nazareth synagogue, He claimed the Spirit prompted prophecy concerning His messianic ministry (Luke 4:14, 18). All the above suggests that we are to anticipate a Spirit energized endeavor.

One illustration will suffice. "It is only by Beelzebub," His protagonists explained, "that this fellow drives our demons" (Matt. 12:24). "If Satan drives out Satan, he is divided against himself," Jesus responded. "But it I drive out demons by the Spirit of God, then the kingdom of God has come upon you" (vv. 26, 28).

The extended role of the Spirit in Jesus' mission is highlighted by Paul's reference to *the Spirit of Christ* (Rom. 8:9). "The chief idea is that the Spirit unites the objective achievement of Christ's sacrifice of atonement to the lives of believers. The Spirit integrates and internalizes the work of Christ with the response of faith."[89]

Chaos imagery abounds. Jesus as light dispels the darkness; He as the vine bears fruit; He as foundation sustains the building; He as life triumphs over death. In each connection, the Spirit bears witness to the truth.

(9) *Spirit in* community. When the day of Pentecost had come, what seemed as tongues of fire rested on *each* of them, and they were *all* filled with the Holy Spirit (Acts 2:3-4).

> The outpouring of the Spirit extended to *all* believers, in contrast to the more selective application of the Spirit to certain persons in the former dispensation. The result was also viewed as more permanent, pervasive, and effective--so much so that nothing previous could be submitted as a genuine parallel.[90]

Reference to their speaking in tongues seemingly recalls the confusion of tongues at the tower of Babel (Gen. 11:9).

> The elements of the story are timelessly characteristic of the spirit of the world. The project is typically grandiose; men describe it excitedly to one another as if it were the ultimate achievement--very much as modern man glories in his space projects. At the same time they betray their insecurity as they crowed together to conserve their identity and control their fortunes.[91]

Observing their megalomania, God confused their language and scatted them to the wind. They would be given ample time to reflect on their corporate presumption.

With Pentecost, a token language restoration took place. Each was enabled to hear in his indigenous tongue. Confusion gave way to clarity. God succeeded wherein man had failed.

The messianic community would resemble creation as a symbiotic union. "No organism is an island. Humans as well as tiny protoctists are symbiotic composites. The biological world is a web of organismal interrelationships at different levels of organization."[92] As with the biological world, so also with the social structure. There would be a variety of persons, differently gifted, interacting in amazing complex ways, orchestrated by the Spirit.

By way of elaboration, *mutual symbiosis* is desirable on a biological level, because all components benefit. *Parasitic symbiosis* provides a contrast, where one component benefits at the expense of another.

Mutual symbiosis also better serves the social ideal. The Spirit designed the community so "that its pars should have equal concern for each other. If one part suffers, every part suffers with it; if one part is honored, every part rejoices with it" (1 Cor. 12:25-26).

Paul extended the symbiotic paradigm to public worship. "But everything should be done in a fitting and orderly way" (1 Cor. 14:40). Not to promotes some and diminish others, but so that all might be edified.

As for the tongues of fire, they manifest God's presence. He is in their midst, a Holy God. He is in their midst, to set apart a holy people. Thomas Troegar writes as if in response: "Holy Spirit, Wind and Flame, move within our mortal frame. Make our hearts an altar pyre. Kindle them with your own fire. Breathe and blow upon that blaze till our lives, our deeds and ways speak that tongue which every land by your grace shall understand" (*Wind Which Makes All Winds That Blow*).

(10) *Spirit with a mission.* "All power in heaven and earth has been given to me," Jesus announced. "Therefore go and make disciples of all nations... . And surely I am with you always, to the very end of the age" (Matt. 28:18-20).

As the disciples preached, so they were to live. They were to incarnate their message. They were to involve themselves in *ethical discourse* as evidence of the indwelling Spirit.

Ethical discourse, according to Paul Lakeland, should embody three elements. "In the first place, it must be compassionate and sensitive to the lives or ordinary people in the everyday world. This may not be where the truth lies, but it a *sine quo non* for the truth reaching and convincing its supposed audience."[93]

"Second, there must be a clear progression of ideas from fundamental principles that the entire community would unquestioningly accept to so-called middle axioms (decision and action oriented guidelines) if not to particular applications of these principles." When this is not possible, it should be content with setting forth the fundamental principles.

Third, truth must be sincerely expressed. There must be a high correlation between "the speech-acts of the speaker and action-contexts in which they are embedded." As stated earlier, persons must practice what they preach.

Jesus stated the above in metaphorical manner. "You are the light of the word," He assured the disciples. "A city set on a hill cannot be hidden" (Matt. 4:14).

"Neither do people light a lamp and put it under a bowl. Instead they put it on its stand, and it gives light to everyone in the house. In the same way, let your light shine before men, that they may see your good deeds and praise your Father in heaven" (vv. 15-16). In context of the Synoptic Gospels, they were to expose the light they received concerning the mysteries of the kingdom.

This recalls a story told by J.B. Philipps. It seems that two angels were viewing *the visited planet* from the lofty perspective. A blinding light emanating from the planet caused them to shield their eyes. In a moment it was gone. Darkness prevailed until small lights began to appear, connecting up until the planet was bathed in a soft glow. As one would guess, the birth of Jesus was the brilliant light. While present, He was the light of the world. With His death, darkness resumed. Following His resurrection, the disciples were the small lights joining together to bathe the world in a soft glow.

Jesus described His followers as *the people of light* (Luke 16:8). So they would be both then and now.

In retrospect, the Spirit appears in mission perspective as the *Spirit of light*. He penetrates the darkness. He resists its counterattacks. He persists until history has run its course, and kingdoms of this world surrender to the consummate rule of God.

(11) *Spirit in kingdom context.* In addition to exploring a final concern, this topic allows us to tie loose ends together. The kingdom of God is complex in character. It expresses the sovereign reign of God, His covenant relationship with the Hebrew people, the inauguration of the messianic age, and eventual rule when redemptive history has reached its goal.

From chaos perspective and by way of repetition, the kingdom of God is best expressed in dynamic terms. God turns events to fulfil His benevolent purposes. Whether in one connection or another, kingdom reality reveals an identical weave.

> The Christian welcomed the messianic age with the advent of Jesus, but in its initial stage rather than full consummation. This resembled a time overlap, wherein the present age continued along with the age to come. The vestiges of the present age would finally dissolve with the second advent of Christ.[94]

Meanwhile, the forces of evil would wage a last desperate struggle, only to collapse under the relentless resolve of God.

The Spirit serves the kingdom strategy by sustaining the fallen but not forsaken world, restraining the forces of evil, and promoting the cause of righteous. As concerns the first of these, the prophet recalls: "Because of the Lord's great love we are not consumed, for his compassion never fail" (Lam. 3:22).

As concerns the remaining, the sins of the fathers are visited on their posterity to the third and fourth generation, the benefits of their righteousness extend to a thousand generations (Exod. 20:5-6). Thus is life Spirit skewed to restrain evil and further the good.

"Chaos theory reveals a light that, although we have stepped into it newly, has always shone about us, waiting to be reflected in our minds and, in a new way, in our hearts through a new song of deliberate worship."[95] *The song of the redeemed*!

Part III

Chaos From A Historical Theology Perspective: A Case Study

Historical theology chronicles the demanding task of relating eternal truths to changing situations. It draws upon divine revelation to apply to current situations.

Geoffrey Bromily aptly comments: "It (historical theology) fills the gap between the time of God's Word and the present time of the church's word by studying the church's word in the intervening periods. In so doing it has a triple function."[96] He elaborates in abridged fashion as follows:

(1) It shows how the church and word have negotiated history, and maintained continuity in spite of continuing change.

(2) It provides examples of how the church has either been faithful to God's word or compromised it.

(3) It brings to the church today a valuable accumulation of insights, warnings, and encouragements.

We inevitably build on the foundations laid by others. For our sake and that of succeeding generations, we should take our task seriously. We pick up our responsibility with a classic example: Augustine's *The City of God*. What we learn in this connection will hopefully stand us in good stead in other circumstances.

Chaos theory not only confirms earlier plaudits for Augustine's work, but adds a revealing dimension. Conversely, He seems to anticipate much of what chaos theory documents. This may be as a result of his keen insight, his reliance on Scripture, or most likely a combination of both. As such, he seems as if a person born before his time.

THE CITY OF GOD

"If any work deserves the title of a classic of Christian literature, it is most certainly Saint Augustine's *The City of God*. Critical historians point to it as perhaps the first major philosophy of history, and its influence also spills over into literature, philosophy, and theology."[97] It no less provides us with an exceptional opportunity for bringing chaos theory to bear in the course of church history. In so doing, we will accent earlier commentary, and add to a growing legacy.

The Author

The paradigm of Western theology, Aurelius Augustine (354-430), bishop of Hippo, stands at the close of the early history of Christianity. In his own life experience he encountered all the major problems of the early church and in his writings bequeathed to the future seminal answers that have influenced Christianity and secular thought ever since.[98]

The medieval church and reformers drew heavily on him. So did Kant, Hegel, Marx, and Whitehead, among every so many others. (Of incidental interest, my first paper in graduate school was on Augustine.)

Four controversies shaped Augustine's thought: (1) Manicheism, which led him to reject Gnostic tents about reality and evil, (2) Donatism, which encouraged him to think through the nature of the sacraments and political life, (3) Pelagianism, which elicited his views concerning sin and free will, and (4) paganism, which evoked his philosophy of history. The driving fore in Augustine's life appears to be his intense desire to find happiness (fulfilment). In whatever connection (emotionally, intellectually, and spiritually), success eluded him until he made his peace with God. Or as alternatively stated, God created a vacuum that only He could fill. Even then it was of provisional nature as an earnest of the future.

Augustine was born in Tagaste in North Africa of a pagan father and devout Christian mother. After a thorough education, he plunged into sensual pleasures. He took a mistress at seventeen, who bore him a son at eighteen.

In 373 Augustine became associated with Manicheism. It was a syncretistic religion containing elements of Gnosticism, Zoroastrianism, Buddhism, and Hinduism. It proposed an elaborate myth in which light struggled with darkness. Man was created by the demons to trap light (the soul). Deliverance could be achieved through ascetic practices.

After nine years as a Manichaen, Augustine became a skeptic. For one thing, the Manichaen myth seemed increasingly implausible. For another, simple Christian monks seemed better able to control their passions than he. It was during this period that he prayed: "Make me chaste and continent, O Lord, but not yet."

Neoplationism hurried Augustine's departure from Manichaenism, and continued to impress him even after his conversion to Christianity. It may be characterized as an *emanistic pantheism*. As such, it looked upon the world as an overflow, a diffusion of the divine life, and reabsorption as the final goal of existence. The stages in the overflow are spirituality, animality and corporeality; of reabsorption sensible perception, reasoning, and mystical intuition.

In 384 Augustine accepted an appointment to teach rhetoric in Milan, and there came under the influence of Ambrose, a man of letters, bishop, and persuasive orator. He was primed to believe by what he heard, and driven to believe by his inability to control his passions. Whereupon, burdened with guilt, he fled into a garden sanctuary. There he heard a voice saying *take up and read*. He opened his Bible at random to read: "Let us conduct ourselves becomingly as in the day, not in reveling and drunkenness, not in debauchery and licentiousness, not in quarreling and jealously. Put on the Lord Jesus Christ, and make no provision for the flesh, to gratify its desires" (Rom. 13:13-14). He felt a sense of peace. His life was transformed. The next Easter eve he was baptized by Ambrose on confession of his faith.

With the death of his mother (388), Augustine returned to Tagaste with friends to set up a monastery. He was ordained in 391, and four years later he became the ruling bishop of Hippo. By 400 he completed his *Confessions*, recording his profoundly moving spiritual odyssey.

Augustine took on the Donatist controversy in connection with his ecclesiastical office. The Donatists held that the sacraments were invalid if performed by unworthy clerics. Since theirs was the only church to rigorously maintain purity, they reasoned that only they were the true church and only their sacraments were efficacious.

As for Augustine, he argued for the validity of the sacraments as such. While only saints comprise the true church, the empirical church is comprised of both saints and sinners. It is a condition which must be tolerated, as confirmed by Jesus' parables. Taking his reasoning a step further, Augustine encouraged the state to use force against both Donatists and heretics. Coercion, he concluded, might be used for good or evil.

The third controversy to shape Augustine's thinking was with Pelagianism. Pelagius, a learned lay monk from Britain, arrived in Rome about 385. He was shocked by the immorality he witnessed on seemingly every hand. He firmly believed in free will, and our ability not to sin. He reasoned that God would not give us commands that we were unable to keep.

Augustine's experience convinced him that one cannot overcome sin simply by wishing to do so. Evil is much too powerful an adversary for us. We need divine intervention.

Conversely, we do not merely sin; we are sinners. Once disoriented by sin, the will is powerless to re-assert itself. Thus we would remain but for the grace of God. "In God's bestowal of grace, faith conquers ignorance, love displaces self-centeredness, and hope triumphs over death."[99]

Finally, there was paganism. Alaric, commander of the West Goths, after two previous efforts sacked Rome in 410. The event had reverberations throughout the empire. The *pax Romana*, symbol of order, had collapsed. Chaos swept over the empire as if raging flood.

Certain erudite Romans fleeing to North Africa set out to blame the Christians for Rome's collapse. They supposed this was do to the populace turning from the traditional gods.

Augustine took it upon himself to answer their charge in the *City of God*. He began writing his *magnum opus* in 412, and finished it in 426. The latter date was only four years before his death, and at a time when the Vandals were besieging Hippo.

In the first five books, Augustine refutes the pagans' argument. In the second five, he suggests that pagan religion is a poor investment in eternity. The two, taken together, are decidedly polemic. Books 11-14 trace the rise of two cities: the divine and human, 15-18 their course, and 19-22 their termination. These comprise an understanding of history that incorporates chaos within a confident faith.

In retrospect, seldom have so many been indebted to one person. Augustine's monumental contribution has withstood the ravages of time. It is as relevant today as when written.

The Impetus

The *pax Romana* was a social wonder of the ancient world. Aelius Aristedes of Smyrna, reflecting on this phenomenon, appreciatively wrote:

> A man simply travels from one country to another as though it were His native land. We are no longer frightened by the Cilician pass or by the narrow sandy tracks that lead from Arabia into Egypt. We are not dismayed by the height of mountains, or by the vast breadth of rivers or by inhospitable tribes of barbarians. To be a Roman citizen, nay even one of your subjects, is sufficient guarantee of personal safety.[100]

Chaos was thereby thought held at bay. "On the huge capitals of the columns, the emperor himself is shown as Zeus destroying the Titans, represented by snake-headed monsters. The provincials were expected to see him as their protector against evil and the forces of chaos that always threatened their existence."[101]

All this changed with drastic suddenness. The impossible had happened. Rome had fallen.

How was one to explain this tragedy? Nero had on a previous occasion blamed the Christians for the destruction making way for his building project. Now they were introduced again as the culprits deserving condemnation for depreciating the patron deities.

Augustine would rather have deferred to others to answer the challenge. None were forthcoming. Reluctantly he took up the task, sensing its high priority for the time in which he lived.

It led him to larger things: a description of two graphically described city, a profound philosophy of history, and a penetrating description of life. As a result, it spoke not only to that time but all times; not simply concerning one incident but all.

It remains to took at *The City of God* in some detail. Not merely as a classic in Christian literature, philosophy of history, or theological treatise, although it qualifies in all these connections. More to the point, it serves to illustrate how chaos theory enriches the understanding of our theological legacy.

One Through Five

Augustine sets out to refute his protagonists' claim that Rome's fall could be explained (in a simple causal manner) as resulting from neglect of its patron deities at the instigation of Christians. In chaos retrospect certain features of his defense seem especially relevant. These testify to his keen insight into the persisting character of life as we experience it.

First, we consider how Augustine approached chaos *per se.* His Roman protagonists, as noted above, viewed the *pax Romana* as a barrier against chaos. There was some measure of truth to this perception, although it was seriously overdrawn. This should have been evident, if not before, once the empire lay prostrated before the invading barbarians. Theirs was not an altogether novel experience: empires wax and wane with the passing of time, and as impacted by developments--both external and internal.

Augustine discloses the error in their thinking in various connections. For one, he underscores the fact that their experience was not unique. "All the spoiling, then, which Rome was exposed to in the recent calamity--all the slaughter, plundering, burning, and misery--was the result of the custom of war" (I.7). Those who take up the sword will perish by it. Persons reap, all things considered, what they sow.

For another example, the pagans were manifestly inconsistent.

> Hence the injuries you do, you will not permit to be imputed to you; but the injuries you suffer, you impute to Christianity. Depraved by good fortune, and not chastened by adversity, what you desire in the restoration of a peaceful and secure state, is not the tranquility of the commonwealth, but the impurity of your own vicious luxury (I.34).

Otherwise, they would appreciate the pervasive character of evil. For every man, however laudably he live, yet yields in some points to the lust of the flesh. Though he do not fall into gross enormity of wickedness, and abandoned viciousness, and abominable profanity, yet he steps into some sins, either rarely or so much the more frequently as the sins seem of less account (I.9).

This leads to a related consideration: the moral parameters God puts on life. Augustine bitterly complains: "We would ask why their gods took no steps to improve the morals of their worshipers. ...Surely it was but just, that such are as men showed to the worship of the gods, the gods on their part should have to the conduct of men" (I.2).

In chaos theory, "Bounded (the setting of parameters) means that on successive iterations the state stays in a finite range."[102] As applied to this instance, the moral order does not deviate except as applied to particulars. Man must conform to God's moral law or suffer the severe consequences. God makes no exceptions.

Along a different line of reasoning, Augustine senses the self-similar (fractal) character of life. We have already noted this concerning the rise and fall of successive nation states. They wage war, not primarily for benevolent purposes, but for its spoils. Then, when ravaged by others, they look around for a plausible scape-goat. In this instance, the Christians. More recently, the Nazis singled out the Jews to blame for their troubles.

This fractal imagery can be illustrated in another manner. That is, with regard to the church as a sanctuary. "But what was novel, was the savage barbarians showed themselves in so gentle a guise, that the largest churches were chosen and set apart for the purpose of being filled with the people to whom quarter was given, and that in them none were slain, from them none forcibly dragged" (1.7). No doubt Augustine meant to call attention to the actual situation, but in a larger sense to suggest the self-similar character of mother church. It ever serves as a sanctuary for time and in prospect of eternity.

For some, moral determinism seems in conflict with free agency. It brings to mind a comment from chaos theory: "You know the old adage 'you can't have it both ways'--well, in mathematics, sometimes you can."[103] It also appears that in theology sometimes you can.

Augustine keeps returning to God as sovereign creator, with implications for His continued providential activity. Here, too, he resembles recent chaos theorists. Barry Parker for instance observes: "From this tiny nucleus the universe was born in an instant of unimaginable chaos. All the particles of nature--electrons, protons, quarks, and so on--came, at least indirectly from this explosion."[104]

"Where did the energy that produced this come from?" Parker asks in rhetorical fashion. Two hundred pages later he sums up: "Creation depends on the basic laws of nature--without them it would not be possible. Who created these laws? There is not question but that a God will always be needed."[105]

Augustine comments as follows: "God, the author and giver of felicity, because He alone is the true God, Himself gives early kingdoms both to good and bad. Neither does He do this rashly...but according to the order of things and times, which is hidden from us, but thoroughly to Himself" (IV.33). It is not that God is subject to such order, he adds, but "rules as lord and appoints as governor."

We will touch on one other matter in this context. Augustine confirms what the religious sociologist Peter Berger refers to as the *rumor of angels*. That is, an awakening awareness of the supernatural. Joe Rosen reasons as follows:

> Since science cannot authoritatively speak about the universe as a whole, we have here an opening for the legitimate entry of nonscientific modes of comprehension into the business of explaining the material universe. Here one's feelings and beliefs can be just as valid as the scientific-appearing descriptions espoused by scientists.[106]

He and others refer to this expanded rationale as the *anthropic principle*, that man may in the framework of science provide a key to the character of life.

If so, this may suggest a shift in paradigm. Thomas Kuhn has effectively documented how science corrects itself by shifting from one paradigm to another by way of successive stages: weakening of the prevailing paradigm, tentative experimentation with another, and consolidation of the latter.[107] He also warns us that the shift characteristically creates vigorous denial as an evidence that the previous model has hardened into cultural dogma.

While Augustine has pressed his argument forcefully, he concludes this section on a conciliatory note as concerns Roman piety. "So also these despised their own private affairs for the sake of the republic, and for its treasure resisted avarice, consulted the good of their country with a spirit of freedom, addicted neither to what their laws pronounced to be crime nor to lust" (V.15). They thereby deserve our recognition, appreciation, and emulation.

Books Six Through Ten

Augustine now goes on the offensive, castigating the pagan gods and those who would derive from them temporal advantage to the exclusion of eternal felicity. "The real causes of worldly catastrophe stem from assertions of arrogant pride and self-sufficiency, seen first in the revolt of angels and then in human rebellion. God is the source of all good, but in the Fall Adam wilfully turned to himself, to the world of creatures."[108] Disoriented, humanity now can achieve only relative good, as illustrated above concerning Roman piety.

The ultimate good, expressed in connection with eternal life, eludes our grasp except for the grace of God. "But God grants grace to a selected few who, in directing their love toward God, form the heavenly city. The two cities, commingled in this world, view with each other throughout history, but in the church the city of God has begun its fulfillment."[109]

"So, then, He only who give true happiness gives eternal life, that is, an endlessly happy life" (VI.17). We search in vain until satisfied in Him. Augustine's personal experience serves as a painful case in point.

The bishop subsequently delves into pagan mythology to demonstrate the impotency of the gods. Since they have difficulty managing life for themselves, they can hardly be expected to intercede on behalf of others. They appear as blind leaders of the blind.

Augustine turns his attention to such religious philosophers as deny the one, true God. Herewith he is more appreciative and conciliatory. He urges them: "let Him be sought in whom all things are secure to us, let Him be discovered in whom all truth becomes certain to us, let Him be loved in whom all becomes right to us" (VIII.4). This advice resembles that of Paul to the erudite Athenians: "And he is not served by human hands, as if he needed anything, because he himself gives all men life and breath and everything else. ...God did this (raised Jesus) so that men would seek him and perhaps reach out for him and find him, though he is not far from each one of us" (Acts. 17:25, 27).

The death/resurrection contrasts with pagan myths in that the former took place in fact rather than religious fantasy. It relates to the real world, where chaos and order jostle for position. It ought therefore to appeal to those who take events seriously, and seek to govern their lives accordingly. Augustine encourages such to walk with him in the pilgrimage of faith.

He again lashes out at those who invoke the assistance of demons, and thereby reject God's provision of an intermediary.

But if, as is much more probably and credible, it must needs be that all men, so long as they are mortal, are also miserable, we must seek an intermediary who is not only man, but also God, that, by the interposition of His blessed mortality, He may bring me out of their mortal misery to a blessed immortality (IX.15).

Whereas the demons deceive us, God speaks the truth without equivocation.

The good angels seize higher ground. "It is very right that these blessed and immortal spirits, who inhabit celestial dwellings, and rejoice in the communications of their Creator's fulness, ...since they compassionately and tenderly regard us miserable mortals...do not desire us to sacrifice to themselves, but to Him" whom they themselves worship (X.6).

Thus they encourage us to embrace the parameters God places on our existence. Unlike Adam, we ought not presume to exalt ourselves unduly. As stated in the *Westminster Confession*, we should glorify God, and thereby enjoy His presence for ever.

This does not make the pilgrim immune from adversity, but generates a contrasting response to others. While the latter become bitter and recriminate (as with Augustine's adversaries), he learns to trust God for His provision, and cultivates faith along with thanksgiving. Augustine perhaps had in mind Paul's triumphant refrain:

> No, in all these things we are more than conquerors... . For I am convinced that neither death nor life, neither angels nor demons, neither the present nor the future, nor any powers, neither height nor depth, nor anything else in all creation, will be able to separate us from the love of God that is Christ Jesus our Lord (Rom. 8:37-38).

In any case, he feels assured that nothing happens to us in life that God cannot turn to our advantage. If time will not suffice, then God will make it right in eternity. He is no person's debtor.

Books Eleven Through Twenty-Two

Augustine turns his attention from refuting the charge laid against Christians to a comprehensive understand of history that underscore's his rationale. History has for him a beginning, an end, and a pivotal point. It begins with creation, concludes with divine judgment, but peaks with the advent of Christ. God has the lead role, the remainder no more than bit-actors. He continues to address each succeeding generation, while we speak our lines and make way for others.

Origin of two cities (11-14). Anticipating chaos theory, Augustine exhibits a keen awareness of the importance of initial conditions to the dynamics of life. We have on other occasions referred to this in terms of a *strange reactor*. It is thought *strange* since the results are unpredictable, and a *reactor* concerning sensitivity to initial conditions. The more the change, the more the evidence of a common denominator.

Augustine is prompted by Scripture. The Biblical narrative commences: "In the beginning, God... ." This corresponds, as mentioned in an earlier connection, with the Egyptian *time of the gods*, except for the fact that God appears in solitary splendor. He had no rivals.

We are thus primed to view the pagan deities as usurpers. Whatever their origin, they appear as alien to life. They offer nothing more than an escape from reality.

God created the world, and it was without reservation good. He created mankind as the climax of creation. Male and female, He created them in His image, to have communion with Him, and to act as steward over His larger creation. He would be tempted to reach higher, and settle for less-- neither of which would satisfy the original purpose.

After this, the serpent made its appearance. As noted earlier, a serpent connotes various things in antiquity and subsequently. Perhaps most persistent, it implies deception. It is in this connection that an Arab villager will wiggle his hand back and forth, in contrast to a straight line, to emphasize that a person cannot be trusted. Along with deception, the serpent is dangerous; his bite can be lethal. Then, too, it is associated with chaos. Offer hospitality to the serpent, and chaos will follow as certain as the night follows the day.

As noted above, Augustine traces the two cities to "two diverse and contrary communities of angels, in which the origin of two human communities is also found" (XI.34). Man falls prey to a conflict already in progress. He appears at times as little more than a pawn in a cosmic conflict. On other occasion, he seems the chief perpetrator of suffering.

"For there is nothing so social by nature," Augustine concludes, "so unsocial by its corruption, as this race. And human nature has nothing more appropriate, either for the prevention of discord, or for the healing of it...than the remembrance of that first parent of us all...that all men might thus be admonished to preserve unity among their whole multitude" (XII.27). The contrast is striking: social by nature, and unsocial by corruption! The admonition is apt: recall our common lineage and seek reconciliation with one another.

From chaos perspective, *bifurcation* characterizes the commingling of the two cities. *Bifurcation* implies a division, with a doubling of possibilities. One could readily illustrate this with a computer and proper software. The results would be impressively complex, with sensitivity to initial conditions.

"Accordingly," Augustine comments, "two cities have been formed by two loves: the earthly by the love of self, even to the contempt of God; the heavenly by the love of God, even to the contempt of self. The former, in a word, glories in itself, the latter in the Lord" (XIV.28).

It does not follow that we should hate ourselves. Quite the reverse! It is as we love God that we come to appreciate ourselves as created in His image. It is also as we love God that we recognize others created in His image. Love, from Augustinian perspective, needs to be prioritized.

Course of two cities (15-18). It remains to run the program. Augustine approaches the earthly city more in generic terms, the heavenly city more with specific instances derived from Scripture. The earthly city waxes and wanes. It constructs from the spoils of war, for the purpose of self-indulgence, and thereby sows the seeds of its own destruction. Temporal good can postpone the day of reckoning, even as evil hastens it, but neither alters the end result.

Augustine nonetheless qualifies as follows: "But the things which this city desires cannot justly be said to be evil, for it is itself...better than all other human good. For it desires earthly peace for the sake of enjoying earthly goods, and it makes war in order to attain to this peace" (XV.4). Even so, the "pursuit of such, to the neglect of the heavenly, reaps misery." Thus would he encourage us to set our affections on eternal verities.

Godliness is a mystery to us except as illustrated in Scripture. Herein we have the account of those who walked by faith, and for us to emulate. Such as those who

> through faith conquered kingdoms, administered justice, and gained what was promised; who shut the mouths of lions, quenched the fury of the flames, and escaped the edge of the sword; whose weakness was turned to strength; and who became powerful in battle and routed foreign enemies (Heb. 11:33-34).

The righteous walk not be sight but faith. They have a goal but no road map. They do not know what the future holds, but Who holds the future. John Polkinghore reflects as follows:

> I would like to suggest, respectfully, that when God came to create the world, he faced a dilemma. God is faithful, and the natural gift of the faithful God will be reliability in the operation of his creation. However, reliability itself could harden into mere rigidity, leading to a clockwork world in which

nothing really new ever happened.[110]

In fact, God is also loving, and as such grants His creatures freedom to act within constraints. We understand this as parents. There comes a time when the child must be allowed to go off on its own, experience life (both good and bad), and hopefully mature in the process.

> There are two extreme pictures of God's relationship to creation that are unacceptable to Christian theology. One is the picture of the universe as God's puppet theatre, in which he pulls every string and makes all creatures dance to his tune alone. The God of love cannot be such a cosmic tyrant.[111]

But no less can he be understood as an indifferent spectator, who leaves mankind to self-destruct. Freedom within constraints and reliability are both gifts of God, and life ingredients.

The termination of two cities (19-22). We are not so much pushed by the past, as Jurgen Multmann would often remind us, but pulled by the future. Or as the pandit observed: "We were given eyes on the front rather than rear of our head." So that would look forward.

"Augustine conceives of God saving individuals, not political regimes, for the Christian's home is not in this world where coercive power prevails. Yet Christians are not to abandon worldly affairs; they are to submit to political authority. They are to help mitigate iolence, sin, and injustice."[112] In these and other ways, they are to function as righteous catalysts.

"If, then, we be asked what the city of God has to say upon these point," Augustine insists, "it will reply that life eternal is the supreme good, death eternal the supreme evil, and that to obtain the one and escape the other we must live rightly" (XIX.4). "When we mortals possess such peace as this mortal life can afford, virtue, if we are living rightly, makes a right use of the advantages of this peaceful condition; and where we have it not, virtue makes a good use even of the events a man suffers" (XIX.14). "But this is true virtue," Augustine continues, "when it refers all the advantages it makes a good use of, and all that it does in making good use of good and evil things, and itself also, to that end in which we shall enjoy the best and greatest peace possible."

Death is not the end. After death, there is still God to be reckoned with. We need not fear the severity of God's judgment, but its justice. But for His grace, none would escape damnation.

Hell, according to C.S. Lewis, is that which God prepares for those who will receive nothing better from Him. As for heaven, Augustine appears virtually overwhelmed by its prospects. "Doubtless this passeth all understanding but His own," he concludes. "But as we shall one day be made to participate, according to our slender capacity, in His peace, both in ourselves, and with our neighbors, and with God our chief good" (XXII.29).

How will all this come about? We allow Polkinghorne to speculate: "The history of the universe is the story of a gigantic tug of war. On one side is the effect of the Big Bang, driving the matter of the world apart. On the other side is the relentless pull of gravity, trying to make things come together."[113] If the former prevails, great black holes will form within each galaxy and eventually decay into low-grade radiation. "This way, the world ends in a dying whimper."

If, on the other hand, the latter wins out, we are no better off. "What began with the Big Bang will end in the Big Crunch as all matter falls back into a cosmic melting point. This way, the world ends in a bang." Whimper or bang, it matters little. Life in the long run would appear futile if this is all there is to it.

Since Polkinghorne is convinced that there is something more, he turns our attention to Jesus' rebuke of the Sadducees as to their understanding of God. "He is not the God of the dead," Jesus affirmed, "but of the living" (Mark 12:27). "The point is that if Abraham, Isaac and Jacob mattered to God once--and they certainly did--they mattered to him for ever. The same is true of you and me. ...Our belief in a destiny beyond our death rests in the loving faithfulness of the eternal God."[114]

This is not, Polkinghorne assures us, a hope void of verification. "Christian belief in a destiny beyond death has always centered on resurrection, not survival. Christ's Resurrection is the foretaste and guarantee, within history, of our resurrection, which awaits us beyond history."[115] "If Christ has not been raised," Paul asserts, "our preaching is useless and so is your faith. ...But Christ has indeed been raised from the dead, the firstfruits of those who have fallen asleep" (1 Cor. 15:14, 20). Augustine would heartily concur.

"The *City of God* is a book about 'glory'. In it, Augustine drains the glory from the Roman past in order to project it far beyond the reach of men, into the 'Most glorious City of God'."[116] Life ends, according to the erudite and pious bishop, not with a whimper or bang but glory. The glory of God, in which the faithful will participate. It is not as a result of merit they have accumulated, but by the grace of God.

Augustine deserves a final word. "I think I have now, by God's help, discharged my obligation in writing this large. Let those who think I have said too little, or those who think I have said too much, forgive me; and let those who think I have said just enough join me in giving thanks to God" (XXII.30). I would ask as much but no more for my present efforts.

ENDNOTES

1. Heinz-Otto Peitgen, Hartmut Jurgens, and Deitmar Saupe, *Chaos and Fractals*, p. 656.
2. Gordon Wenham, *Genesis 1-15*, pp. 15-16.
3. Derek Kidner, *Genesis*, p. 44.
4. Robert Seltzer, *Jewish People, Jewish Thought*, p. 197.
5. Edgar Peters, *Chaos and Order in the Capital Markets*, p. 204.
6. Kidner, *op. cit.*, p. 91.
7. Ibid., p. 101.
8. John Durham, *Exodus*, p. 7.
9. Charles Pfeiffer, *Old Testament History*, p. 133.
10. Christoph Barth, *God with Us*, pp. 14-15.
11. R. Alan Cole, *Exodus*, p. 69.
12. Ibid., p. 70.
13. Dale Aukerman, *Reckoning with Apocalypse*, p. 200.
14. Gordon Wenham, *Numbers*, p. 120.
15. Xavier Leon-Dufour, *Dictionary of Biblical Theology*, p. 98.
16. R.K. Harrison, *Numbers*, pp. 217-218.
17. Robert Gordes, *Poets, Prophets, and Sages*, p. 54.
18. Leon-Dufour, *op. cit.*, p. 100.
19. Yohanan Aharoni, *The Land of the Bible*, p. 8.
20. Walter Brueggemann, *First and Second Samuel*, p. 57.
21. Gleason Archer, *Encyclopedia of Biblical Difficulties*, p. 170.
22. Pfeiffer, *op. cit.*, p. 237.
23. Simon DeVries, *I Kings*, p. xxv.
24. Daniel Kaplan and Leon Glass, *Understanding Nonlinear Dynamics*, p. 27.
25. Ralph Klein, *Israel in Exile: A Theological Interpretation*, p. 3.
26. Raphael Patai, *Man and Temple*, p. 132.
27. Morris Inch, *My Servant Job*, p. 9.
28. David Clines, *Job*, p. 21.

29. Ivars Peterson, *Newton's Clock: Chaos in the Solar System*, pp. 1-2.
30. Inch, *op. cit.*, p. 36.
31. Ibid., p. 76.
32. Morris Inch, *A Case for Christianity*, p. 132.
33. Andre Neher, *The Exile of the Word*, p. 21.
34. Pfeiffer, *op. cit.*, p. 564.
35. Ibid., p. 586.
36. Joyce Baldwin, *Haggai, Zechariah, Malachi*, p. 252.
37. Helena Nusse and James Yorke, *Dynamics: Numerical Exploration*, p. 269.
38. F.F. Bruce, *Romans*, p. 159.
39. Luke Johnson, *The Gospel of Luke*, p. 79.
40. R. Alan Cole, *Mark*, p. 111.
41. Michael Field and Martin Golubitsky, *Symmetry in Chaos*, p. 161.
42. Helmut Thielicke, *Theological Ethics*, vol. 1, pp. 3-4.
43. For an extended discussion of the ethical implications of discipleship see Morris Inch, *Exhortations of Jesus According to Matthew* and *Up from the Depths: Mark as Tragedy*, pp. 1-61.
44. Barry Parker, *Chaos in the Cosmos*, p. 84.
45. Simon Kistemaker, *Hebrews*, p. 265.
46. William Johnsson, *Defilement and Purgation in the Book of Hebrews*, p. 157.
47. Donald Guthrie, *New Testament Theology*, p. 446.
48. Hendrikus Berkhof, *Christian Faith*, pp. 395-396.
49. Arthur Nock, *Early Gentile Christianity and Its Hellenistic Background*, p. 2.
50. Ibid., p. 3.
51. John Stott, *The Gospel and the End of Time*, p. 94.
52. George Ladd, *A Commentary on the Revelation of John*, p. 277.
53. Parker, *op. cit.*, p. 288.
54. Ibid., p. 289.
55. Ibid.
56. Ian Percival, "Chaos: A Science for the Real World," *Exploring Chaos* (Hall, ed.), p. 16.
57. Walter Brueggeman, *Living Toward a Vision*, p. 22.
58. Jaques Marquet, *The Aesthetic Experience*, p. 131.
59. Glen Tinder, *The Political Meaning of Christianity*, p. 163.
60. Brueggeman, *Living Toward a Vision*, p. 111.
61. Tinder, *op. cit.*, p. 35.
62. John Paulos, *Beyond Numeracy*, p. 33.

63. James Bleick, *Chaos: Making a New Science*, p. 251.
64. Gordon Wenham, *op. cit.*, pp. 72-73.
65. Donald Bloesch, *Freedom for Obedience*, p. 107.
66. Paulos, *op. cit.*, p. 34.
67. Tinder, *op. cit.*, p. 42.
68. Bloesch, *op. cit.*, p. 141.
69. R.K. Harrison, *Jeremiah and Lamentations*, p. 74.
70. Richard Bauckham, *The Bible in Politics*, pp. 48-49.
71. Ibid., p. 50.
72. Gleick, *op. cit.*, p. 252.
73. Peter Coveney, "Chaos, Entropy and the Arrow of Time," *Exploring Chaos* (Hall, ed.), p. 212.
74. Paulos, *op. cit.*, p. 86.
75. Brueggeman, *Living Toward a Vision*, pp. 162-163,
76. Peters, *op. cit.*, pp. 133f.
77. Percival, *op. cit.*, pp. 11-21.
78. Harrison, *op. cit.*, p. 73.
79. Norman Gottwald, *The Tribes of Israel*, pp. 677-678.
80. Wenham, *op. cit.*, p. 12.
81. Morris Inch, *Saga of the Spirit: A Biblical, Systematic, and Historical Theology of the Holy Spirit*, p. 18.
82. Ian Steward, "Portraits of Chaos," *Exploring Chaos* (Hall, ed.), p. 149.
83. Wenham, *op cit.*, pp. 144-145.
84. Donald Hagner, *Matthew 14-28*, p. 719.
85. Donald Hagner, *Hebrews*, pp. 187-188.
86. Gleich, *op. cit.*, p. 252.
87. Walter Kaiser, *Toward an Old Testament Theology*, p. 81.
88. R.T. France, *Matthew*, p. 95.
89. James Edwards, *Romans*, p. 205.
90. Inch, *Saga of the Spirit*, p. 85.
91. Kidner, *op. cit.*, p. 109.
92. Vernon Ahmadjian and Surinder Paracer, *Symbiosis*, p. 1.
93. Paul Lakeland, *Theology and Critical Theory*, pp. 178-179.
94. Inch, *Saga of the Spirit*, p. 76.
95. David Steenburg, "Chaos at the Marriage of Heaven and Hell," *Harvard Theological Review*, 1991, 84 (4), p. 466.
96. Geoffrey Bromily, *Historical Theology: An Introduction*, p. xxvi.
97. Frank Magill (ed.), *Masterpieces of Christian Literature*, vol. 1, p. 141.

98. Clyde Manchreck, *A History of Christianity in the World*, p. 67.

99. Ibid., pp. 73-74.

100. Aelius Aristedes, *Oratio*.

101. W.H.C. Frend, *The Rise of Christianity*, pp. 165-166.

102. Daniel Kaplan and Leon Glass, *Understanding Nonlinear Dynamics*, p. 27.

103. Michael Field and Martin Golubitsky, *Symmetry in Chaos*, p. 161.

104. Barry Parker, *Creation*, p. 10.

105. Ibid., p. 202.

106. Joe Rosen, *The Capricious Cosmos*, pp. 3-4.

107. Thomas Kuhn, *The Structure of Scientific Revolutions*.

108. Manchreck, *op. cit.*, p. 75.

109. Ibid.

110. John Polkinghorne, *Quarks, Chaos, and Christianity*, p. 41.

111. Ibid., p. 42.

112. Manchreck, *op. cit.*, p. 76.

113. Polkinghorne, *op. cit.*, p. 90.

114. Ibid., p. 92.

115. Ibid., p. 93.

116. Peter Brown, *Augustine of Hippo*, p. 311.

BIBLIOGRAPHY

Aharoni, Yohanan. *Land of the Bible*. Philadelphia: Westminster, 1979

Ahuradjian, Vernon and Surinder Paracer. *Symbiosis*. Hanover: University Press of New England, 1986.

Archer, Gleason. *Encyclopedia of Bible Difficulties*. Grand Rapids: Zondervan, 1982.Aristedes, Aelius, *Oratio*.

Augustine, Aurilius. *The City of God*. New York: Modern Library, 1950.

Aukerman, Dale. *Reckoning with Apocalypse*. New York: Crossroad, 1993.

Baldwin, Joyce. *Haggai. Zechariah, Malachi*. Leicester: Inter-Varsity, 1972.

Barth, Christoph. *God with Us*. Grand Rapids: Eerdmans, 1991.

Bauckham, Richard. *The Bible in Politics*. Louisville: Westminster/John Knox, 1989.

Berkhof, Hendrikus. *Christian Faith*. Grand Rapids: Eerdmans, 1979.

Bloesch, Donald. *Freedom for Obedience*. San Fransisco: Harper and Row, 1987.

Bromiley, Geoffrey. *Historical Theology: An Introduction*. Grand Rapids: Eerdmans , 1978.

Brown, Peter. *Augustine of Hippo*. New York: Dorset, 1986.

Brueggemann, Walter. *First and Second Samuel*. Louisville: John Knox, 1990.

_____. *Living Toward a Vision*. Philadelphia: United Church, 1988.

Bruce, F.F. *Romans*. Leicester: Inter-Varsity, 1992.

Carter, Ben. *Unity in Diversity*. Lanham: University Press of America, 1991.

Clines, David. *Job*. Word: Waco, 1889.

Cole, R. Alan. *Exodus*. Leicester: Inter-Varsity, 1973.

_____. *Mark*. Leicester: Inter-Varsity, 1991.

Coveney, Peter. "Chaos, Entropy and the Arrow of Time," (*Exploring Chaos*, Hall ed.), pp. 203-212.

DeVries, Simon. *I Kings*. Word: Waco, 1889.

Durham, John. *Exodus*. Word: Waco, 1987.

Edwards, James. *Romans*. Peabody: Hendrickson, 1993.

Field, Michael and Martin Golubitsky. *Symmetry in Chaos*. Oxford: Oxford Univesity, 1992.

France, R.T. *Matthew*. Grand Rapids: Eerdmans, 1985.

Frend, W.H.C. *The Rise of Christianity*. Philadelphia: Fortress, 1985.

Gleick, James. *Chaos: Making a New Science*. New York: Viking, 1982.

Gordes, Robert. *Poets, Prophets, and Sages*. Bloomington: Indiana University, 1971.

Gottwald, Norman. *The Tribes of Israel*. Maryknoll: Orbis, 1979.

Guthrie, Donald. *New Testament Theology*. Downers Grove: Inter-Varsity, 1981.

Hagner, Donald. *Hebrews*. Peabody: Hendrickson, 1993.

_____. *Matthew 14-28*. Dallas: Word, 1995.

Hall, Nina (ed.). *Exploring Chaos*. New York: Norton, 1991.

Harrison, R.K. *Jeremiah and Lamentations*. Leicester: Inter-Varsity, 1973.

Inch, Morris. *A Case for Christianity*. Wheaton: Tyndale, 1997.

_____. *Exhortations of Jesus According to Matthew* and *Up from the Depths: Mark as Tragedy*. Lanham: University Press of America, 1997.

_____. *My Servant Job*. Grand Rapids: A Discussion Guide on the Wisdom of Job. Baker, 1985.

_____. *Saga of the Spirit: A Biblical, Systematic, and Historical Theology of the Holy Spirit*. Grand Rapids: Baker, 1985.

Johnson, Luke. *The Gospel of Luke*. Collegeville: Liturgical, 1991.

Johnsson, William. *Defilement and Purgation in the Book of Hebrews*. Ph.D. diss., Vanderbilt University, 1973.

Kaiser, Walter. *Toward an Old Testament Theology*. Grand Rapids: Zondervan, 1991.

Kaplan, Daniel and Leon Glass. *Understanding Nonlinear Dynamics*. Berlin: Springer-Verlag, 1995.

Kidner, Derek. *Genesis*. Leicester: Inter-Varsity, 1967.

Kistemaker, Simon. *Hebrews*. Grand Rapids: Baker, 1984.

Klein, Ralph. *Israel in Exile: A Theological Interpretation*. Philadelphia: Westminster, 1979.

Kuhn, Thomas. *The Structure of Scientific Revolutions*. Chicago: University of Chicago Press, 1970.

Ladd, George. *A Commentary on the Revelation of John*. Grand Rapids: Eerdmans, 1972.

Lakeland, Paul. *Theology and Critical Theory*. Nashville: Abingdon, 1990.

Leon-Dufour, Xavier. *Dictionary of Biblical Theology*. New York: Seabury, 1973.

Magill, Frank (ed.). *Masterpieces of Christian Literature*, 2 vols. New York: Salem, 1963.

Manshreck, Clyde. *A History of the Christian World*. Englewood Cliffs: Prentice-Hall, 1985.

Neher, Andre. *The Exile of the Word*. Philadelphia: The Jewish Publication Society of America, 1981.

Nock, Arthur. *Early Christianity and Its Hellenistic Background*. New York: Harper, 1964.

Parker, Barry. *Chaos in the Cosmos*. New York: Plenum Press, 1996.

_____. *Creation*. New York: Plenum , 1988.

Polkinghorne, John. *Quarks, Chaos, and Christianity*. New York: Crossroad, 1997.

Patai, Raphael. *Man and Temple*. New York: KTAV, 1947.

Paulos, John. *Beyond Numeracy*. New York: Knopf, 1991.

Peitgen, Heinz-Ott, Hartmut Jurgens, and Dietmar Saupe. *Chaos and Fractals*. Berlin: Springer-Verlag, 1992.

Percival, Ian. "Chaos: A Science for the Real World," (*Exploring Chaos*, Hall, ed.), pp. 11-21.

Peters, Edgar. *Chaos and Order in the Capital Markets*, New York: Wiley, 1991.

Peterson, Ivars. *Newton's Clock: Chaos in the Solar System*. New York: Freeman, 1993.

Pfeiffer, Charles. *Old Testament History*. Grand Rapids: Baker, 1973.

Rosen, Joe. *The Capricious Cosmos*. New York: Macmillan, 1991.

Seltzer, Robert. *Jewish People, Jewish Thought*. New York: Macmillan, 1980.

Steenberg, David, "Chaos at the Marriage of Heaven and Hell," *Harvard Theological Review*, 1991, 84 (4), pp. 448-466.

Steward, Ian. "Portraits of Chaos," (*Exploring Chaos*, Hall, ed.), pp. 44-58.

Stott, John. *The Gospel and the End of Times*. Downers Grove:

InterVarsity, 1991.
Thielicke, Helmut. *Theological Ethics*. 3 vols. Grand Rapids:
    Eerdmans, 1979.
Tinder, Glen. *The Political Meaning of Christianity*. New York:
    Harper/Collins, 1991.
Wenham, Gordon. *Genesis 1-15*. Word: Waco, 1987.
_____. *Numbers*. Leicester: Inter-Varsity, 1981.

INDEX

ark, 7-8, 60-61, 94, 96

anthropic principle, 111

basin of attraction, 47

bifurcation, 47, 114-115

blessings, 8-9, 11, 16, 20, 25, 36, 40-41, 97, 112, 116

bondage/oppression, 11-14, 43-44

boundries (parameters), vi, 5-6, 8, 32, 40-41, 48, 83, 110, 113

chaos/randomness, vi, 3-4, 8-9, 21, 23-24, 27, 29, 37, 39, 51, 71, 77-78, 80-81, 85, 89, 91, 96-97, 107

   chaos paradigm, vi, 20, 89

   chaos theory, vi-vii, 3, 6, 13, 21, 32, 73, 80, 85-86, 102-103

church, 59-61, 96, 99-101, 103, 106-107, 110

community, 15-16, 28-29, 44, 59-61, 99-101

covenant, 8-9, 15, 20, 28-31, 68, 96-97

creation, 3-6, 77-80, 89-94, 110, 113-116

determinism/design, 4, 8, 21, 24, 81, 90, 110, 116

disciples, 51-54, 63-64, 69-70, 86, 100-101

ethical discourse, 100-101

faith, 7, 15, 24, 41, 48, 51, 60, 69, 78-79, 82, 86, 107, 115, 117

faithfulness of God, 7, 24, 78-79, 92, 95-96, 115-117

fractals, vi, 8, 20-21, 52-54, 73, 110

grace, 5, 13, 29, 41-42, 59, 72, 80, 88, 107, 112, 116

Holy Spirit, 3, 9, 89-102

hope, 15, 20, 33, 36, 42, 67-69, 107, 116-117

idolatry, 4, 11-12, 23, 27, 31, 108-114

iteration, 32-33

Jesus/Christ, 13, 17, 31, 47-49, 64-65, 68, 87, 97-102, 106, 113, 117

   Christ the center, 48, 101, 113

justice, 53, 79, 85, 115-116

kingdom of God, 17, 24, 36, 54, 79, 87, 101-102, 110-111

love, 53, 60, 68, 84-88, 90, 92, 101, 107, 112-113, 115-116
mankind 4-6, 77-88, 97, 111, 114
mercy, 24, 53, 79, 84, 92, 95
middle axioms, 100
obedience, 8, 21, 23-24, 31-32, 82, 97, 107
order, 4, 8-9, 16, 20, 68, 71-72, 78, 80, 85, 91, 96, 107
providence, 6, 8, 40-41, 78-79, 85-86, 95-97, 110
redemption/deliverance, 6, 12-13, 16, 43, 48, 56, 60, 84-88, 97-102,
    106
referents (allusions to chaos), 4, 72
    darkness, 4, 56, 63-65, 68, 72, 90-91, 95-96, 98, 100
    death, 4, 39, 45, 49, 56, 68, 72, 82-83, 95, 98, 106, 116
    silence, 4, 43-45, 72, 97
    waters (sea), 4, 7-8, 51, 59-61, 68, 72, 95-96
    wilderness, 15-17, 78, 87, 98
resurrection, 49, 56, 101, 112, 117
reverence/fear, 21, 39, 86
righteousness/holiness, 7, 19, 24, 36, 39-42, 56, 68-69, 79, 96, 100-
    101, 115-116
sacrifice, 28-29, 35, 55-57, 98
sensitivity to initial conditions (strange attractors), vi, 4, 7, 32, 73, 80-
    81, 113-114
serpent, 82, 113-114
shalom (peace), 43, 53, 69, 79, 97, 106, 115, 117
    pax Romana, 108-109
sin/evil, 5-6, 20, 23, 27-28, 32, 67, 78, 80-84, 94-97, 102, 107, 109-
    110, 115
    original sin, 5-6, 80, 113
sinister possibilities, 52
suffering/pain, 7, 35-36, 39-42, 52, 60, 68, 87, 93-94, 109, 112, 115
symbiosis, 99
systems, 15
    deterministic systems, 37 (see determinism/design)
    dynamic systems, 4, 21, 24, 32, 39, 102
    natural systems, 5-6, 19-20, 40, 47, 81
    nonlinear systems, vi, 14, 40, 47, 73, 81-82, 89
    systems' maintenance, 25, 27-30, 85
theology, vii, 73, 77, 116
    Biblical theology, vii, 1-2, 75
    historical theology, vii, 103

systematic theology, vii, 75-76
transciency, 93-94
vocation/stewardship, 4, 25, 78-79, 117-118
wrath, 6-7, 16, 20, 79, 80-84, 94-97